Leaders, Executive Coaches, Authors, Educators, Parents, and Students Endorsing *Managing Thought*

"Self-help books, most of us know, are a dime a dozen. This is a self-help book that makes the rest of them obsolete. Mary Lore, through a multitude of pointed vignettes and just plain old common sense, puts the quandary of human existence into a fresh, colorful, and detailed perspective. After my forty years of professional experience in this field, this is the best yet. In short, it is life changing. Most refreshingly, as you read it, you know that the author practices it in her everyday life. Her book is the definitive 'First in Class' on this subject and will go down as a true classic for many years to come!"

Dr. Harry S. Dennis, III
Chairman and CEO, The Executive Committee
Dedicated to increasing the effectiveness and
enhancing the lives of chief executives

"*Managing Thought* will dramatically improve how you think and do. I wish I had read it when I was twenty-five. It's an easy-to-read, yet deeply insightful, interpretation that shows how to manage your thoughts to be more successful. Just the short, effective paragraph on 'Putting it into Practice' will convince you that this is a must-read!"

Kraig Kramers
CEO, speaker, executive coach, and author of *CEO Tools*

"In life, each of us is required by the dynamic reality of daily events to face ourselves or not. We all have the choice to be actively in the game of life or, by default, to stay on the sideline. This book can initiate the process of personal work and consistent focused self-development. My forty years of working with graduate students and CEOs confirms the importance of daily routine in individuals moving toward being brave personally, giving themselves permission to know themselves, and moving beyond the 'other-directed' orientation of critical self-critique. An inner-directed path will allow the growth of a more developed personhood. Mary's book can give its readers the path toward a centered self-confidence."

W. Lynn Tanner, Ph.D.
President and CEO, TEC Canada
Canada's preeminent organization for the development of CEOs

"Bottom-line improvement comes through people, and I want people on my team who can think for themselves, visualize outcomes, and be proactive in seeking positive results. Mary Lore shares a very creative approach to analyzing and measuring our thought process. It validates the importance of being in control to effect positive outcomes in our lives. *Managing Thought* is a must read if you want to develop a personal flight plan that has positive outcomes, takes you to new heights, avoids significant turbulence, and puts you in control."

Howard Putnam
Former CEO, Southwest Airlines
Author of *The Winds of Turbulence*

"*Managing Thought* gets right to the bottom line on why individuals and organizations behave the way they do. *Managing Thought* provides the tools that empower us to learn how to change our behavior and improve our effectiveness and overall health at work and home. I'm a better person, leader, friend, father, and husband for having read this book."

William Neale, MA
Cofounder, Denison Consulting
Developer of diagnostic tools designed to bring
culture and leadership to the bottom line

"*Managing Thought* is to this century what *How to Win Friends & Influence People* and *The 7 Habits of Highly Effective People* were to the last century. Thought management is a key asset for today's leaders."

Barbara G. Stanbridge
Change Management Expert
President National Association of Women Business Owners (2001)

"*Managing Thought* is one of the best self-help books I have ever read. It is thought-provoking and easy to understand, and the exercises are simple yet very effective. Through *Managing Thought*, I now see how my limiting beliefs have held me back and put me in a very small box as to the possibilities in my life. By taking the time to really work on uncovering what they are and examining them in detail, I am able to take myself out of that very small box and help my clients to do the same."

Bob Carrothers
Executive coach, Vistage International
The world's leading chief executive organization

"*Managing Thought* is as timeless as Dale Carnegie's work. This book goes way beyond business executives. It is a powerful book for anyone, in any number of personal and professional relationships. Through *Managing Thought*, I have taken control of my life with powerful, high-service, and high-purpose thoughts. I learned I have the power to choose my thoughts and overpower my weak, negative ones."

Arthur Horwitz
President and CEO, Jewish Renaissance Media,
The leading gatherer and disseminator of information
for and about the American Jewish community

"For years, great leaders have realized 'the power of positive thinking.' Even pessimistic people prefer to follow positive, optimistic leaders. This book takes this concept to a completely new level and teaches us how to actually manage our thoughts to be creative, inspired, and impactful in all that we do. The concepts are practical and real and are equally beneficial at home or in the workplace. Lore's book reinforced that I actually have a choice and can control my thoughts versus being controlled by them—I find that to be incredibly powerful!"

Gordon Krater, CPA
Managing Partner, Plante & Moran, PLLC
One of *Fortune*'s "100 Best Companies to Work For"
for ten consecutive years

"Every outcome in the universe is preceded by an initiating thought. Mary J. Lore's latest book, *Managing Thought*, reminds us and provides the tools to be intentional and aware of our thoughts as they create our reality, to consciously create each moment, and to seek balance in a world that forces us to specialize. Read this book, do what she suggests, and discover more of who you really are. Let your journey begin!"

Ole Carlson
Author of *Beneath the Armor* and
Clarity: Creating a Life That Really Matters . . . to You

"In today's 24/7 global world, executives and entrepreneurs are challenged in all aspects of their professional and personal lives. Today's business education is about teaching future leaders how to manage these challenges. *Managing Thought* provides important and valuable insights as well as robust and realistic prescriptive techniques that will help train business students to overcome those challenges while reinvigorating their passions and cultivating their all-important sense of self."

Kim Schatzel
Dean, College of Business
University of Michigan-Dearborn

"Lore's book reinforced my belief that life is a combination of one's heart, mind, and soul, and when these three are combined and made available to us, along with a grounded understanding of our beliefs, we have the possibility of living life to the fullest."

Richard Carr
Vice Chairman of the Board, Vistage International
The world's leading chief executive organization

"Anything you want in life such as health, a fulfilling career, or happiness begins with a single thought, yet how to manage your thoughts toward your objectives remains elusive to most people. Likewise, while no life is free from troubles, your mind can be trouble-free when you practice self-awareness, self-mastery, and being on purpose. In *Managing Thought*, Mary Lore has done a wonderful job presenting an accessible, step-by-step process for cultivating and reshaping your mind to finally actualize the life you want. A highly recommended book for anyone looking to achieve their life's potential."

Dr. Maoshing Ni, Ph.D., D.O.M.
Cofounder, Tao of Wellness & Yo San University
Author, *Secrets of Longevity* & *Secrets of Self-Healing*

"The guidance of Mary Lore's book, *Managing Thought* turns possibility and learning into daily action. It provides teaching and parenting tools for ourselves, our children, and our world's future."

Bette D. Moer
Founder/director, Cedar Crest Academy & Early Childhood Center

Managing Thought

Managing Thought

Think Differently.
Think Powerfully.
Achieve New Levels of Success.

MARY J. LORE

NEW YORK | CHICAGO | SAN FRANCISCO | LISBON | LONDON
MADRID | MEXICO CITY | MILAN | NEW DELHI | SAN JUAN
SEOUL | SINGAPORE | SYDNEY | TORONTO

The *McGraw-Hill* Companies

1 2 3 4 5 6 7 8 9 0 DOC/DOC 1 9 8 7 6 5 4 3 2 1 0

ISBN: 978-0-07-170341-3
MHID: 0-07-170341-1

This publication is designed to provide accurate and authoritative information in regard to the subject matter covered. It is sold with the understanding that the publisher is not engaged in rendering legal, accounting, or other professional service. If legal advice or other expert assistance is required, the services of a competent professional person should be sought.
—*From a Declaration of Principles Jointly Adopted by a Committee of the American Bar Association and a Committee of Publishers and Associations*

McGraw-Hill books are available at special quantity discounts to use as premiums and sales promotions, or for use in corporate training programs. To contact a representative, please visit the Contact Us pages at www.mhprofessional.com.

This book is printed on acid-free paper.

Dedication

*To all of you
who are changing the world
by changing yourselves*

CONTENTS

INTRODUCTION..1

1. THE SIGNIFICANCE OF MANAGING
    THOUGHT AND THE MOMENT 6

2. HOW DO YOUR THOUGHTS
    RULE YOUR WORLD?...11

3. WE ARE NOT OUR MINDS 16

4. INFINITE CALM BRINGS
    IMMEDIATE RESULTS...22

5. OUR FEELINGS ARE KEY INDICATORS.........................28

6. THE MANAGING THOUGHT PROCESS.........................35

7.   DECIDE WHAT I WANT 40

8. DESTRUCTIVE AND DISEASED THOUGHTS................ 55

9. THOUGHTS THAT WASTE TIME, ENERGY,
    AND MONEY AND BLOCK TRUE REALITY................... 66

10. DISCOVERING AND RELEASING LIMITING
    PERCEPTIONS AND BELIEFS 90

11. HOW TO SHAPE THOUGHT 116

12. CHOOSING MY INTENTIONS 124

13. ASKING POWERFUL QUESTIONS................................ 150

14. MAKING POWERFUL STATEMENTS............................ 174

15. REPLACING WEAK THOUGHT PATTERNS
    WITH POWERFUL THOUGHT PATTERNS.....................190

16. DAILY CULTIVATION 199

17. MANAGING ENERGY 203

18. MANAGING SPIRIT 214

19. MANAGING THOUGHT: PUTTING IT
INTO PRACTICE 225

20. ENJOY THE JOURNEY 237

ACKNOWLEDGMENTS 247

ABOUT THE AUTHOR 251

ABOUT MANAGING THOUGHT 253

We are what we think.
All that we are
arises with our thoughts.
With our thoughts
we remake the world.

—The Buddha

INTRODUCTION

S ince 2002, I have shared the *Managing Thought* process with hundreds of groups throughout North America as a service to Vistage International, also known as TEC, the preeminent international organization that supports the personal and professional development of CEOs and key executives. Participants in these workshops have invited me to share *Managing Thought* with groups of couples, parents, teens, teachers, students, professionals, non-professionals, executives, nonexecutives, and salaried and hourly workers. These participants have written and phoned to tell me how *Managing Thought* profoundly impacted their lives and their relationships with colleagues, direct reports, bosses, customers, friends, spouses, family members, and, most important, themselves.

This book documents the principles of *Managing Thought* and provides a system to apply to any aspect of your thinking and being, such as your life, relationships, family, career, role at work, company, department, vacation, a project, process, opportunity, problem, goal, strategy, or even a telephone call.

This book is filled with information to help you increase your self-awareness and shape your thoughts to accomplish what you want in each moment and live the life you intend. You may find yourself wanting to implement everything immediately. You can relax, because you don't have to. You can choose to practice *just one thing* throughout the moments of your day, and experience a significant transformation in your work and life. Throughout the book, I point out each *just one thing* that you can choose to practice.

Before I embark on a learning experience, I find it helpful to make an assessment of where I am right now. Along the way, I measure, acknowledge, and celebrate the changes I have made and chart my next steps. For this reason, I have developed an assessment for you to measure how you are managing your thoughts right now. If you like, you can take the assessment before reading this book, after you have read this book, and periodically in the future as you continue to practice changing the way you think.

To take the free "How Do Your Thoughts Rule Your World?"® self-assessment, visit www.managingthought.com. It is simple and straightforward and takes about ten minutes. When you are finished, you can print a report and receive guidance on the best steps to take next.

I have written this book so that you can choose the approach to reading that best suits you. For example, you can read it in one or two sittings, then choose a specific topic to focus on. You can read a chapter a day, a week, or a month and play with what you have learned. You can read just a few pages each day. Do what is comfortable for you.

Although it may be tempting, try not to rush through the book. If you have time to mindfully read one page, then read one page and choose one thing to practice and personally experience.

Before you begin to read, take a moment to calm yourself and open yourself to your higher awareness. Take a few deep breaths, relax your neck, massage your scalp, rub your ears, smile, stretch, and loosen your clothing.

You may find yourself thinking all kinds of thoughts as you are reading the book. When your brain tells you, *I've heard that before,* and asks you to put the book down, say, *Thanks for sharing,* and keep reading. When your brain tells you, *Hey, this self-awareness stuff is uncomfortable,* and asks you to put the book down, again say, *Thanks for sharing,* and stick with it. For many of us, transformation is not comfortable. If your brain criticizes or judges you because you should have already known a particular point or because you did know it and failed to practice it and thus wasted time or money or damaged a relationship, again say, *Thanks for sharing,* and keep reading. We are always wiser today than we were yesterday, so it naturally follows that we probably would have said or done something differently had we known then what we know now.

Remember, we learn quickly and achieve significant results when we're in a state of vision and purpose, wonder and possibility, thankfulness, joy, calm, and happiness. In these states, we are inspired and in touch with our creative power. This is not so when we are in a state of criticism, blame, judgment, or anger about ourselves or others.

When you turn on a light in a room, do you get upset that the room was dark before? When you are upset, not only do you miss out on the joy of learning, you cut yourself off from your creative power, your ability to inspire and be inspired, and your ability to access your higher awareness and learn effectively. If you find yourself tempted to criticize or judge yourself as you look at the mirror within, know that you have flipped the switch. Enjoy the light.

Please note that in *Managing Thought,* you do not become someone else. As you become self-aware and on purpose, you are rediscovering your true nature. It is as if you are peeling an onion—peeling away the layers of beliefs, expectations, and ways of thinking and being that you have built up over the years. You are getting back to who you really are, reopening your connection with your higher awareness. You are reconnecting with your strengths and what inspires you—what truly brings you happiness. You are reconnecting with your purpose and passion.

Managing Thought represents thousands of years of wisdom from many roads—business, psychology, biology, chemistry, physics, neurology, metaphysics, and spiritual teachings. Every concept offered serves as an example, and although the experiences of others can be illuminating, they cannot replace your own experience. Although the experiences of others can tell you where a path leads, they do not release you from the duty of taking the path yourself and even changing the path. The more openly and freely you experiment with what is offered in this book, the more you gain as you enjoy the freedom to be you.

I invite you, now, to experience the joy of peeling away all the layers of your humanity and bringing to light your power, your beauty, your gifts, your talents and your purpose in living—your true nature, your authentic self.

Managing Thought
is a journey.
You are invited
to take the journey.

1

THE SIGNIFICANCE OF MANAGING THOUGHT AND THE MOMENT

There is no such thing as the future. The future is an illusion. What we have is a *now*, followed by a *now*, followed by a series of *nows*.

We do not suddenly become bankrupt. We have a series of bankrupt *now* moments. We do not suddenly become a great leader, a great parent, or healthy. We do not suddenly accomplish a goal or fulfill a resolution. We have a series of great leaders, great parents, or healthy *now* moments. When we have experienced enough of these moments, goals are accomplished, bad habits are broken, and resolutions are fulfilled.

It is the same with achieving a great attitude, thinking positively, being engaged, accessing creativity, practicing thankfulness, changing our beliefs, focusing on what we want, creating powerful intentions, fulfilling our purpose, and living our passion—all the things that we

We achieve results by focusing on the moment.

are told we must do to achieve success and fulfill our dreams. And it's the same with being happy, at peace, inspired, creative, and true to ourselves and making a difference. It doesn't happen suddenly. It happens as we build a critical mass of these *now* moments.

We achieve results by focusing on the moment. And the results we achieve—bad, good, or significant—depend on what we focus on in the moment.

Through my experience at work and in life over the last thirty years, I have found that what makes a great leader, a great organization or family, and a great human being are the very same principles. In other words, the keys to success in life and work are the same.

These keys are self-awareness, self-mastery, and being *on purpose.* I define being *on purpose* as focusing your thoughts and actions on what is truly significant to you. Without self-awareness, self-mastery, and being on purpose, we live each day as we did yesterday. And then a year goes by, two years,

> *Without self-awareness, self-mastery, and being on purpose in the moment, we live each day as we did yesterday.*

five years, and then ten, and we wonder what happened. We have the same frustrations and experiences over and over with different jobs, partners, customers, coworkers, employees, children, and spouses. Essentially, we continue to make the same mistakes.

We read books, listen to speakers, and attend courses and seminars to help us learn the best practices, the latest management techniques, systems, processes, methods, and ways of thinking. In most cases, although we say we want to implement what we learned, we don't. We go back to the hustle and bustle of our work and life without making any changes. Sometimes we do implement a change, and it works for us—for a time. Then the going gets tough, and we revert to the familiarity of our previous behavior. Or perhaps we do gain some permanent improvement, yet it's minimal.

How is it that while we want to change, we rarely do? Or when we do, it's a mediocre change, not a transformation? It is because many of us are taught that our actions and our behavior drive results.

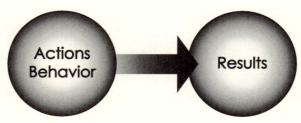

We learn that if we want to change results, we must change our actions. That's what management is all about—changing actions, behavior, processes, and systems. That is also what New Year's resolutions are all about—changing our actions to lose weight or achieve a goal. Thus indoctrinated, we focus on modifying action and behavior as a means of improvement.

The empowering discovery about *Managing Thought* is this: What goes on inside our heads is what drives results.

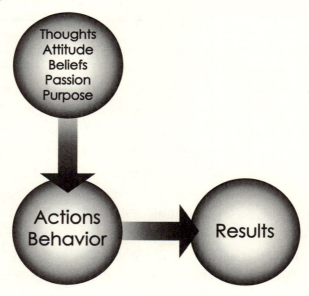

Our beliefs, perceptions, attitudes, intentions, passion, purpose—our thoughts—drive our actions. If we don't address our thoughts, meaningful change does not happen. Conversely, when we *do* begin to investigate our underlying beliefs and attitudes and become mindful of our thoughts, true transformation takes place. We can choose to be aware of our thoughts and what lies behind them because they drive our actions and our ability to devise creative ways to achieve significant results. I am not talking about developing rah-rah motivational goals, mission statements, and resolutions. I am talking about developing self-awareness, being aware of our thoughts and feelings and making subtle yet powerful changes that result in ideas, desires, intentions, and ultimately actions that bring us peace and inspire us.

> *We choose to be aware of our thoughts.*

We become inspired when we are in states of happiness, thankfulness, vision and purpose, and wonder and possibility. In these states, we are in tune with our higher awareness and in touch with our creativity. It is when we are inspired that we achieve significant results. It is when we are inspired that we transform.

> *It is when we are inspired that we transform.*

*Great men
are they who see . . .
that thoughts rule the world.*

—Ralph Waldo Emerson

2

HOW DO YOUR THOUGHTS RULE YOUR WORLD?

Everything we say, do, and physically manifest first begins in thought.

First we have an idea—a thought—followed by desire, another thought, followed by intent, another thought, followed by strategy, goals, and plans, more thoughts, until, finally, we act. We say something, do something, physically manifest something, or create something.

How do your thoughts rule your world? How do your thoughts rule your life, relationships, career, organization, and family? Are your thoughts producing positive results, or are they preventing you from growing fully into your potential? Do your thoughts

> *Everything we say, do, and create first begins in thought.*

inspire you, or are they plagued with self-doubt, fear, and worry? Are your thoughts causing you to feel happy and peaceful, or are they causing you to feel stressed and victimized? Do your thoughts result in a life of joy and perfect health, or do they result in a life of pain and suffering? Do your thoughts cause you to live your life the way you want to live it, or do your thoughts paralyze you, undermine your intentions, or sabotage your efforts? Do your thoughts serve you? Or are you helplessly at their mercy?

Most of us would not imagine that in one moment, we can actually change the course of our lives, our families, and our organizations through our thoughts.

When we are ruled by our thoughts, we are usually in reactive mode. We may find ourselves being offended by our customers or employers; snapping at our spouses; resenting competitors, friends, and coworkers; and generally walking around like emotional time bombs. This is because most of us have taught ourselves to rely on certain familiar thought processes. Jerry Wind and Colin Crook, in *The Power of Impossible Thinking: Transform the Business of Your Life and the Life of Your Business*, refer to these processes as "mental models," which are shaped by a combination of genetics, education, and experience. Mental models are not necessarily bad, although they can be limiting. They tend to be reflex actions that are performed without thought. And because they are habitual, they don't lead to growth. They are the mind's version of being set in one's ways.

> *In one moment we can change the course of our lives.*

When we manage our thoughts, we take a proactive approach instead of being led around by our habitual attitudes and self-limiting beliefs. We are able to use our thoughts to proactively affect those very stressful episodes that we formerly reacted to defensively. In doing so, whole new vistas of options emerge and we experience very different results. Instead of wasting our time, money, and energy on reactivity, we focus on what matters to us—the reality we want.

> *By managing thought, we consciously choose our futures.*

This is what the *Managing Thought* process is all about. It liberates us from passive acceptance of our thoughts and frees us from our attachment or fusion to them. It empowers us to live our lives as we want to live them. In other words, by managing thought, we can consciously choose our futures because everything that we think is a matter of choice. There is no situation or person

> *How we behave depends on how we think.*

responsible or to blame for what goes on inside our heads. The quality of our lives, our organizations, our families, and our careers is dramatically impacted by how we think and how we behave. And how we behave depends on how we think.

When we are mindful of every thought we have and every action we take each day, we achieve significant results at work and in life. The following story shows that how we choose to think in any given moment affects our circumstances, our destiny, and our success.

A Golf Lesson

One of my clients was on the golf course with his business partner and the president of their major customer (representing 80 percent of their revenues). At some point in the middle of their round, the customer mentioned that in six months, he planned to take his business to a manufacturer in China. At this disclosure, my client's partner got very angry and played poorly for the rest of the round. His anger and frustration were not restricted to the course. When he got back to the office, he threw things around his workspace, yelled about how badly they were being treated, and predicted that they were going to be screwed by this customer. [In this industry, agreements are often made and contracts drawn with these very large original equipment manufacturers (OEMs), which then do not sign the contract. In this case, two million dollars of

(continued)

inventory owned by my client's customer was sitting on the shop floor, and there wasn't a signed contract to that effect.] He screamed to get the attorneys on the phone to draw up letters demanding the acknowledgment of ownership of that inventory and a signature on the contract.

My client, on the other hand, played well for the rest of the golf round. He immediately shaped his thought to remind himself how thankful he was that his customer valued the relationship so much that he provided six months' notice. He also reminded himself that his company had recently realized that the work they were hired to do for this customer was low-margin work and was not work at which they were world class. They didn't have the nerve to give up business from a customer that made up 80 percent of their revenue base to pursue higher margins and world-class customers. He realized that his customer's decision would force them to make this bold move, and he was excited about the opportunity. He also acknowledged his company's mission in dealing with its customers—be a partner. He thought that it needn't matter whether the customer was new, continuing, or on the way out the door—the intention is to be a partner with customers. So, he asked his customer, "How can we be of service to you? Have you ever transferred business to China before? How can we help?"

Over the next six months, my client worked with his customer to effect a smooth transition for which his company was paid handsomely. At the same time, he focused on securing customers for work for which the company could be world class and could secure a higher margin. At the end of the six months, he and his partner had new, higher-margin clients. Even more significant, the large client ultimately didn't transition all of its business to China. Instead, it kept the higher-margin business with my client, and my client's company ended up with its best year ever.

Would his partner's approach have achieved the same result? No! With the same circumstances, he very well might have embarked on a path of war and lost. He would have then announced, "See! I told you they were going to screw us!" His focus would have become self-fulfilling.

Thinking has become a disease.
It is not so much
that you use your mind wrongly—
you usually don't use it at all.
It uses you.
That is the disease.
You believe that
you are your mind.

—Eckhart Tolle

3

WE ARE NOT OUR MINDS

Most of us believe that we don't have control over our thoughts. To demonstrate the fallacy of this belief, take a look at the following exercise.

EXERCISE

Take a moment to think of an ice cream cone. Think of the type of cone, the kind of ice cream, the number of scoops, the toppings, if any.

Now stop thinking of the ice cream cone.

Instead, think of a puppy—the twinkle in the puppy's eyes, the wagging tail, the squeals of delight, the excitement, the playfulness.

Were you able to do it?

If so, you have just proven that you have control of your thoughts. You were able to stop what you were thinking to think about the ice cream cone. You were also able to stop thinking about the ice cream cone and begin thinking about the puppy.

Can you also see that you are not your thoughts, and you are not your mind? That you are in control of your mind? You chose to think about the ice cream cone. You chose to think about the puppy. You are the observer, the witness, the watcher, and the user of your mind and your thoughts.

> *I am the observer, the witness, the watcher, and the user of my mind and my thoughts.*

Our brains are tools, just as a computer is a tool. They perform many functions: observing, sensing, storing, retrieving, and relaying information. We are not computers. We are not our brains. We are not the tools. We are the ones *using* the tools. In each moment, we are perfectly able to watch our thoughts, to look *at* our thoughts, not *from* our thoughts. We can catch a thought, look at it, and determine whether it is empowering and constructive. In each moment, we have the ability to choose what to do with the thought. Do we identify with or attach to the thought and let it rule our world? Do we let the thought go? Do we rephrase the thought? Or do we take the moment to say

> *Our brains are tools, just as a computer is a tool.*

to our brains, *Thanks for sharing*, and choose thoughts that move us in a direction that serves our purpose?

I have observed that many of us spend much of our lives fused with the reptilian portion of our brains, the oldest and most primitive brain structure, and consequently experience a great amount of pain and suffering.

Have you ever been alone at night and heard an unexpected noise? When you heard the noise, did you stop to listen intently? At that moment, and with amazing speed, your hypothalamus, which is inside the limbic system of the brain, made a decision on your next course of action and provided you with three choices: fight, flight, or freeze. Without self-awareness, when we hear or see something that is different from what we expect, our brains act as if we are in physical danger and present us with fight, flight, or freeze thoughts. We may choose to argue, criticize, judge, complain, blame, act defensively or offensively, or become angry, anxious, or frustrated (fight). Or we may choose to avoid a situation by leaving, denying, or ignoring it, or we may worry, become overwhelmed, experience self-doubt, or feel regret (flight). Perhaps we experience shock and do nothing, or we procrastinate, suffer from depression, or act like victims (freeze). In fact, when the reptilian portion of the brain is activated, the limbic system takes over, and the part of our brain that plans, prioritizes, and evaluates information becomes incapable. When we are not mindful, we unknowingly remain in fight, flight, or freeze; lose sight of our purpose; waste significant time, energy, and money; and achieve less than desirable results. When we are in fight, flight, or freeze, we are completely cut off from our ability to access our higher awareness and creativity.

Before we react, we can pause to observe our thoughts and shape them.

When we manage our thought, we are capable of being aware that our brains are in fight, flight, or freeze and adding another choice. I refer to this choice as *light*. When something happens that is not a life-or-death matter or is not physically unsafe, we can take a moment to add light to the situation. Instead of fighting, fleeing, or freezing, we can practice taking a breath before we react, first exhaling deeply, then inhaling, and utilize that moment to consciously assess the situation. We can pause to observe our thoughts and shape them. This simple action causes our thinking to move from the hypothalamus to the frontal cortex of the brain, where we have a vast array of alternative courses of action. We achieve very different and significant results, as was demonstrated in the story "A Golf Lesson" in the previous chapter. The one man chose fight. The other chose light. Choosing to fight or focusing on light results in dramatically different circumstances.

Through managing our thought, through mindfulness in each moment, we move from the back of our brains to the front of our brains. In doing so, in that moment we reshape our circumstances, remain on purpose, and achieve significant results.

> *Through mindfulness in each moment, we reshape our circumstances.*

I invite you to take the first step of self-awareness and begin to pay attention to your thoughts, noticing them as an observer, without blame or judgment—noticing that a thought is merely a thought. If you were to pick *just one thing* from this book to use, it could be to start watching your thoughts, looking *at* your thoughts, not *from* them, and see what happens. Notice if your thoughts are of fight, flight, or freeze. Notice whether you are buying into your thoughts. See what choices you are making as a result of relying on your thoughts and see if these choices serve your purpose. Practice noticing the

> *Start watching your thoughts. Notice the choices you are making by relying on your thoughts.*

patterns of your thoughts. Without blame or judgment, as an unbiased observer, practice choosing how you might think or react differently the next time a similar situation arises.

A Lesson in Fear

Lily's company had a customer that accounted for over 80 percent of her business. Her team heard that the customer was planning to take the business in-house and become a competitor. Lily received no response to the messages she left for the executives of the company. When I met with Lily, she was experiencing everything her reptilian brain had to offer— fear of losing the business, plotting vindictive courses of action, bothered by their inappropriate behavior, and unable to think about what to do next.

When Lily discovered that the fight, flight, and freeze thoughts of her brain were ruling her world, she immediately decided to stay vigilant in each moment, noticing and saying no to her brain's thoughts of fear, blame, judgment, and being a victim. She encouraged her team to do the same and to consciously wonder about possible courses of action. Immediately, they devised a number of powerful ways to communicate and deal with their customer. They also developed a number of extremely creative ideas on where to take the business, building on their significant strengths and capabilities. The entire team transformed. They were so excited about executing the new strategy that they couldn't wait to transition away from this customer.

When we are in states of fear, blame, judgment, feeling overwhelmed, anger, frustration, and disappointment, it is impossible to be in touch with our creativity. It is impossible for us to be inspired. By consciously choosing to add light to a situation, we open ourselves to our higher awareness and to a state of creativity and clarity. We feel at peace, and we become inspired.

As you practice watching your thoughts, you will find yourself dismissing those which are negative and disempowering. In time, you will find that your thoughts are working for you instead of against you. You will find yourself calm and at peace.

The more tranquil
we become,
the greater is
our success,
our influence,
our power for good.

—James Allen

4

INFINITE CALM BRINGS IMMEDIATE RESULTS

P sychologists estimate that, on average, we have as many as sixty thousand thoughts in a typical day. If we sleep six to eight hours a day, then we are having about one thought each second.

We have sixty thousand thoughts a day.

When I started paying attention to my thoughts, I found my head filled with an endless dialogue. I was surprised to discover that I wasn't having sixty thousand new and useful thoughts. Instead, I was repeating a series of unproductive fight, flight, and freeze thoughts—doubts about myself, doubts about my abilities, imagining upcoming scenarios with difficult people and difficult situations, criticizing and judging myself and others, and analyzing everyone and everything (and not necessarily in a positive way).

If everything we say and do first begins in thought, I wondered how I was able to accomplish anything of significance to me with all that chatter.

I was reminded of a rule often talked about in business called the 80-20 Rule. First observed by Italian economist Vilfredo Pareto in 1906, the rule states that 80 percent of what we do brings home only 20 percent of the value. Although this rule is useful in business, I have found that it applies to practically any human activity, including our thinking. If we want to experience what we truly want, it makes sense to overcome the 80-20 Rule inside our heads. Then all, or at least a much larger percentage, of our thoughts result in the best use of our time, effort, and money, and we achieve what is important to us.

In addition, when we manage our thoughts and stay in the moment, we release many of those sixty thousand daily thoughts. We create the space for powerful thoughts to come through.

Think about it—when do you get your best ideas? When have you made your best decisions? When I ask this in a *Managing Thought* workshop, the answers are universal: *When I am in the shower. When I first wake up. Before I go to sleep. When I am on a walk. When I am running. When I exercise. When I'm driving. When I am relaxing. When I am meditating. When I am doing something I love to do.*

What is in common to these responses? We have cleared our heads of the endless chatter. We are not forcing ourselves to think. We let go of our thoughts,

> *Through managing our thoughts, we become calm and receptive to our creative ideas.*

and in so doing we gain access to our higher awareness and creativity.

Yet what do we do when we find ourselves in a difficult situation? We cancel our vacations, skip lunch, stay late, and work on the weekends, forcing ourselves to come up with the solution. We don't allow ourselves to do what we enjoy doing until we have solved our problems. We are actually making matters worse.

Creative ideas emerge when our heads are clear, when we give our minds a rest, and when we do what we love to do. These creative ideas result in great decisions. And we don't waste time, energy, or money. We focus on what is significant.

Remember, we learn quickly and achieve significant results when we're in a state of vision and purpose, wonder and possibility, thankfulness, joy, calm, and happiness. In these states, we are inspired and in touch with our creative power. This is not so when we are in a state of force.

If you were to choose *just one thing* to practice from this book, the next time you notice that you are forcing yourself to find a solution, take time to be quiet, go for a walk, get some fresh air, exercise, connect with friends and family, do what you enjoy. Before you do, invoke the state of wonder and wonder what your solution might be and see what happens. Before you go to sleep at night, wonder and see what ideas emerge when you awake.

We all have the ability to ask ourselves questions, wonder, and listen for the answers. We discover the right thing to do and how to do it. We find a power within that indeed transforms us. We become inspired and inspire others.

Through managing our thoughts and overcoming the 80-20 Rule, we become calm, peaceful, and receptive to our creative ideas. These creative ideas result in great decisions. We are also able to choose to focus our thoughts on what is significant to us and in so doing make the most of each experience. In this way, we create happiness, peace, and inspiration in each moment.

We can create happiness, peace, and inspiration in each moment.

A Choice Lesson

Jerry told me that he was working harder than he would like. He told me that he had been given the unofficial responsibility of learning how the company's software worked, training his colleagues, and being the expert resource for the company on a national level. In an irritated manner, he said that he had to work more hours and travel to fulfill this responsibility and, as a result, felt exhausted in the evenings.

When Jerry took a moment to become aware of his thoughts, he realized that he didn't *have to* assume this responsibility or work extra hours—he *chose* to. He replaced his *have to* thoughts with *choose* thoughts and in so doing, discovered that his choice was actually consistent with his true nature. This in turn brought about thoughts of peace and empowerment versus thoughts of being forced to do this work. He discovered that he was inspired by his choice because he truly loved learning new things, traveling and meeting people, making presentations, teaching, and being a respected and valued resource. When he became at peace and inspired by his choice—which was aligned with his purpose— he became happy and energized and no longer felt exhausted in the evenings. His creativity was sparked, and ideas came to him on how to further increase his energy. This enhanced his productivity at work and improved the quality of his time spent at home.

In the above story, Jerry was thinking thoughts of blame, judgment, and criticism. He felt like a victim—stuck in *having to* work more hours with no ability to develop creative solutions or to be happy, energized, and at peace. When Jerry changed his *have to* thoughts to *choose* thoughts, he discovered that he was indeed living in a way that truly mattered to him and made him happy. If you were to practice *just one thing* from this book, you could notice each time you think or say *have to* and change it to *choose*. Then see what happens.

Each time you think or say *have to*, change it to *choose*. See what happens.

When we align our thoughts and actions with what truly matters to us, we feel at peace.

In each moment, we can consciously choose thoughts and actions that serve us. When our thoughts and actions are aligned with what truly matters to us, we feel a sense of satisfaction and peace with each moment. When we feel at peace, we have access to our higher awareness, and creative ideas shine through.

In the sphere of feeling,
we can freely experience
what speaks to our soul.

—Rudolph Steiner

5

OUR FEELINGS ARE KEY INDICATORS

You are not your mind, your thoughts, or your feelings.

Many of us believe that feelings have no place at work or in making important decisions. We believe that feelings can get in the way of results. This is not true.

It is not our feelings that cause difficulty. We, in fact, are the cause—acting without self-awareness.

Our feelings are an extremely valuable tool in the workplace and in life. When we choose to be aware of them, they serve as a key indicator of whether—or not—a thought is truly serving our purpose.

Feelings and emotions are simply thoughts manifested in the physical body. When you bring to mind a memory, you probably notice that you begin to experience the feelings and emotions tied to that memory. If you were angry, your nostrils might begin to flare and you might feel the blood rush to your face, just as it did when you had the initial experience.

As we begin practicing *Managing Thought*, it may not be possible for us to be fully aware of all of our thought patterns. It

Our feelings tell us if a thought truly serves our purpose.

may not be possible for us to intellectually know whether a thought is truly powerful for us. Often, it is through the awareness of our feelings that we can bring our thoughts into view. And it is through the awareness of our feelings that we can discover the true power of our thoughts.

Our feelings represent the connection between our mind and our spirit. If there is a conflict between your thoughts and your feelings, it is your feelings that are telling the truth. They are telling you the truth at that moment.

If you don't *feel* right as you think a thought, then use your feelings as a key indicator to help you take further steps in self-awareness and determine whether or not your thoughts truly serve your purpose.

Throughout the book, I ask you to notice how you are feeling as you are thinking a thought. I ask you to say your thought out loud to bring your thought into your physical body so that you can feel it.

Our feelings represent the connection between our mind and our spirit.

Take a moment to test this for yourself. First, exhale deeply. Then inhale to calm your internal chatter. Close your eyes and begin thinking a thought that you know does not work for you. For example, if you know that worry thoughts do not work for you, then imagine you are in a state of worry and begin thinking your worry thoughts. Notice how you feel as you are thinking these thoughts.

What happens to your head and neck? Forehead? Chest and gut? Jaw? Mouth? Eyes? Posture? Energy? Heartbeat? Breath?

Now think about something you are truly thankful for. How do you feel as you are thinking these thoughts of thankfulness? Pay particular attention to what happens to your spirit and your sense of inner power.

Then state aloud the following sentences. As you say each sentence, notice the difference in how you feel. Again, pay particular attention to what happens to your spirit and your sense of inner power.

- I am focused.
- I am focusing.
- I choose focus.
- I choose to focus.
- I have to be more focused.
- I have to focus.
- I need to be more focused.
- I need to focus.
- I should be more focused.
- I should focus.
- I will focus.
- I am going to focus.
- I wonder what I can focus on in this moment.
- What can I focus on in this moment?
- When will I ever be able to focus?
- Why can't I focus?

Which thoughts caused your forehead to crinkle and your eyebrows to furrow? Which thoughts caused your body to tighten? Which thoughts caused a sense of heaviness? A sense of force? Which thoughts caused your face or body to lighten up? Which thoughts felt good? Which thoughts felt powerful? Inspiring?

If you didn't notice a difference, I invite you to close your eyes; take a few deep breaths, focusing on the exhale, to put yourself in touch with your higher awareness; and try it again. You may want to try it with a word other than *focus,* such as *happy* or *organized.*

There is a distinct difference in the power of a thought. It is the powerful thoughts that inspire us, spark creativity, move us in

> *It is the powerful thoughts that inspire us and spark creativity.*

the direction we want, and build momentum.

Right now your brain may be telling you to skip this exercise. Remember, it's just doing its job. It has searched its memory banks and doesn't see that you have ever done this before. It is in fight, flight, or freeze. It decides that this could be dangerous and wants you to avoid danger. So thank your brain for sharing. You may even tell it that it's safe to check this out, and it's interesting and useful to notice these differences.

The thoughts in the critical and forceful column probably caused your eyebrows to furrow and your body to tighten. Your breaths may have shortened, and your heartbeat may have quickened. These thoughts do not bring peace and are not inspiring

THE POWER OF A THOUGHT

Weak Thoughts

Critical and Forceful	Not in the Present	Powerful Thoughts
I have to be more . . .	I have to . . .	I am . . .
I need to be more . . .	I need to . . .	I now . . .
I should be more . . .	I should . . .	I choose . . .
I need to . . .	I will . . .	I am choosing . . .
I should . . .	I am going to . . .	What can I . . . ?
Why can't I . . . ?	I choose to . . .	How can I . . . ?
What should I . . . ?	How will I . . . ?	I wonder what I can . . .
When will I . . . ?	What will I . . . ?	I wonder . . .

because they are thoughts of judgment, criticism, and force. These thoughts actually move you away from what you want because they

> *Thoughts of blame and judgment cut off our ability to receive ideas.*

cut off your ability to access your higher awareness and receive ideas on how you can be what you want to be. Say each sentence out loud and notice what happens.

Thoughts that are not in the present are not powerful because they are not in this moment. They are thoughts of the future, and as we talked about in Chapter 1, there is no such thing as the future. The future is an illusion. True power comes from being in the present, *now* moment. Say each sentence out loud and notice the difference.

The powerful thoughts are powerful because they help us bring about joy, thankfulness, and a state of vision, purpose, wonder, and possibility. They open the door to our higher awareness and let in ideas on how we can be in our moments. Say these out loud and notice the difference in how you feel compared to the thoughts of force or future.

Did you notice that *I choose* is listed as a powerful thought and *I choose to* is listed as weak? *I choose* and *I am choosing* are powerful because they are in the present moment and consistent with what is true to you. *I choose to* is not powerful because it is a thought of the future. Close your eyes and repeat the statements out loud. Notice the difference.

When you find yourself thinking that you can't do or be what you want, or when you are critical of yourself for not having been able to be what you wanted in the past, *I choose* or *I now* may feel more powerful to you than *I am*. When you have absolutely no idea of *how* to focus, for example, *I wonder what I can focus on in this moment* may feel more powerful. It is powerful because you are invoking your creativity by thinking thoughts of wonder.

Restate the thoughts in the powerful column of the chart. Which one brings you the greatest sense of inner power?

If you were to choose *just one thing* to use from this book, it could be this step in self-awareness. Notice how you feel in body and spirit as you think a thought or say it out loud. (For those of you in business, notice how you feel as you state your mission statement or read aloud your e-mails, literature, or other communications with your customers, suppliers, and employees.) Do you feel inspired? Do you feel at peace? Do you feel true to yourself? Do you feel that you can make a difference? Do you feel a sense of wonder? If not, there is another way to think the thought to serve your purpose.

> *Notice how you feel in body and spirit as you think a thought or say it out loud.*

In time, you find yourself dismissing negative, disempowering thoughts. You find that your thoughts are aligned with what is significant to you, working for you and not against you. You find yourself calm and at peace.

Others notice a transformation in you. The tension in your face melts, your shoulders relax, your spine straightens, your chin lifts, and your eyes brighten. You look happy, at peace, and inspired. We observe the real you. The onion is peeled.

Sow a thought,
and you reap an act.
Sow an act,
and you reap a habit.
Sow a habit,
and you reap a character.
Sow a character,
and you reap a destiny.

—Charles Reade

6

THE MANAGING THOUGHT PROCESS

I approach *Managing Thought* as if I were pruning a tree. When I prune a tree, the first thing I do is decide what I want to accomplish. Do I want to remove the dead wood? Create a certain shape? Bring in more light? More fruit or flowers? Growth upward or outward? Once I have my purpose, I begin to prune, first removing the dead and diseased branches. I then prune the branches that are crossing other branches, sticking straight up, or shooting from the base of the tree. These are appropriately called suckers because they suck up the water, nutrients, and sunlight from the viable branches. Once these branches are removed, I prune and shape the tree to fulfill my purpose. After completing the process, I turn my attention to the daily cultivation of the tree—how it is fed and watered and its exposure to the elements. This helps the tree resist stress and develop a strong root and trunk system. With less stress, the tree resists insects, disease, and damage. It thrives in its full glory.

With less stress, a tree resists insects, disease, and damage. It thrives in full glory. It is the same for us.

To manage thought, we can follow the same process. Before we plan or strategize anything—a career, vacation, marriage, education for ourselves or our children, a corporate initiative—we can decide what we want. Before we say or do anything, such as interact with our family, children, or significant others or converse with a customer or coworker, we decide our purpose. We decide what is of significance.

Then we watch our thoughts and prune those which are destructive and diseased. These thoughts do not bring us peace or inspire us. We notice and prune the thoughts that are at cross-purposes, or sucking up our time, energy, and money. These are the thoughts that block our light—our true reality. We practice shaping our thoughts, creating our intentions, and focusing our thoughts, and ultimately our actions, on what matters to us. In doing so, we accomplish our purpose and fulfill our intention in each moment. We cultivate ourselves daily and develop a strong mind, body, and spirit. We resist stress, disease, and damage. We thrive in our full glory.

The following chapters of this book take you through the *Managing Thought* process by continuing to use our pruning analogy.

SELF-AWARENESS

Know Thyself.

—Socrates

*I can teach anybody how to get
what they want out of life.
The problem is that I can't find anybody
who can tell me what they want.*

—**Mark Twain**

7

DECIDE WHAT I WANT

The title of this chapter may sound like a simple thing to do, yet in working with myself, individuals, families, and organizations, I have found that deciding what we want can be an extraordinarily difficult thing to do. Some of us think it's selfish to decide what we want and even worse to get it. Some of us think it's impossible to get what we want. Others are afraid of deciding the wrong thing. Others elect to play it safe and don't decide anything.

Most of us haven't thought about what we want.

What I see most often is that we simply have not thought about it. We haven't taken a moment to reflect and decide what we want. When we live each day as we did yesterday, busily going through each day by rote, we don't stop to think about if what we are thinking, saying, or doing results in what we really want. This is the 80-20 Rule in action.

You may have heard it said, "If you don't know where you are going, any road will get you there." Unfortunately, most of us don't know where *there* is, even when we've arrived.

What Thomas *Really* Wanted

Thomas is a business owner who is blessed as a visionary and who aspired to greatness for his company. As such, he was a frustrated man. Even though he tried to implement all the right systems, apply the right management and growth techniques, and hire the right people for the critical positions in the firm, his business continued to languish at mom-and-pop status. He could never take a vacation, or if he did, he spent most of his valuable vacation time on the phone, managing the day-to-day activities of the company, which could have been easily handled by his managers.

If you were to ask Thomas what he wanted, he probably would have told you, "I want my business to grow to world-class status, and I want to be able to take a decent vacation without constant interruptions." In our work together, I asked him to investigate his desires even more deeply. I asked him what it was that he really wanted. In other words, what would world-class status and a decent vacation bring to him? At this point, the realization came to him that what he really wanted in his life was joy. He related how his wife got up each morning nearly bursting into song out of pure joy. That was what he wanted. This realization occurred at the end of January. At the beginning of May, Thomas arrived at our meeting looking like a new man. His posture was erect; his stride was confident and relaxed. Even his face seemed to glow. Typically, we start our meetings by reporting our level of wellness in our professional and personal lives on a scale of one to ten. In the past, Thomas had usually reported numbers in the five and six range. That day, he gave two tens as his numbers.

As Thomas focused on experiencing joy in the moments of his life, including moments at work, other compartments of his day-to-day existence fell into place. In this short time, he hired people and put processes in place that raised his company to world-class status. He took a two-week vacation and didn't *have* to call the office once. By focusing on the essence of what he wanted—joy—Thomas was able to access his higher awareness and *know* the right systems to implement and the right people to hire. When we are able to access our higher awareness, we know the right thing to do.

Most of us spend a lot of time thinking and talking about what we don't want or what we don't like. Unfortunately, thinking and talking about what we don't want does not define what we do want. *I don't want to be in debt. I don't want to fight anymore. I'm tired of working so hard. I hate my job. I don't like my life. I need to lose weight. The economy is bad. I don't like this or that about my employees, my customers, my suppliers, my kids, or my spouse.* These thoughts do not define what you *do* want. Even worse, these thoughts set in motion a destructive chain of events that leads to the very reality that you are attempting to avoid.

> *Thinking and talking about what we don't want does not define what we do want.*

What Jennifer *Really* Wanted

Jennifer worked in a successful law firm and one day learned that she was in the running for managing partner—a dream come true for many lawyers. Jennifer found herself surprised by her reaction to the news. She was thinking that she didn't want to be the managing partner. As she explained her reasons for not being managing partner, she noticed at least twenty perceptions affecting her view of the reality of being managing partner. She said that previous managing partners lost their balance: they worked an excessive number of hours, they lost their sense of play and fun, the firm became their priority, their family lives suffered, they had to retire when their tenure was completed, and their interest in the well-being of the associates and clients gave way to their interest in the profitability of the firm seemingly at all costs.

Upon reflection, Jennifer could see that everything listed represented what she didn't want. She had not dedicated any thinking to what she did want. She remembered the 80-20 Rule and realized that although these changes of lifestyle and management style might be true for most managing partners, they do not have to be true for her. She can manage her thoughts, strategy, plans, and actions to align with what is significant and of value to her. She really did want to serve as the managing partner, and she wanted balance. With these thoughts, her doubts faded and she became inspired.

We may criticize ourselves because we don't have balance, or we may worry about not having financial security. If we have not defined what balance looks like or what financial security means, then thoughts of criticism and worry rule our world and we have no way of knowing how to get there. When we are in states of blame, judgment, fear, criticism, and worry and not in states of joy, thankfulness, vision and purpose, or wonder and possibility, it is impossible for us to be in touch with our higher awareness. It is impossible for us to develop creative ideas on how to be balanced or to achieve financial security. Even worse, we may have no way of seeing that we may already be there.

For example, many of us spend our day criticizing our situations at work—customers, suppliers, bosses, subordinates, team members, and so on. Often, if we take a moment to think about what we want from our work, we discover that we have many opportunities to fulfill what we want during our day. If we ask ourselves, *If work was ideal, what could it bring to me?* we bring to our awareness what we want from our work that truly matters to us. For example, if we are aware that learning is what we want, we become able to notice all the moments at work from which we can learn. Instead of criticizing someone, we might ask questions to learn and gain a wider perspective. Or we might reflect on how we might do things differently if we find ourselves in similar situations at some point in the future. If teaching is what we want, instead of criticizing others for their ignorance or stupidity or getting upset about how much time it takes to explain something, we

> *If we take a moment to think about what we want, we discover that we have many opportunities to fulfill what we want during the moments of our day.*

> *As soon as we know what we truly want, we become incredibly creative in seeing the possibilities.*

could notice these moments as an opportunity to share and to teach. Often, as soon as we know what we want (and it is true to who we are), we become incredibly creative in seeing the possibilities to live the way we want in our current situation or in a new situation. When we do not know what we want and are unable to experience the moments of what we want because we cannot see them, we continue to have the same experiences and complaints again and again, year after year.

Now it is time to ask yourself, *What do I want?*

This may be a difficult question for you to answer right now. If your brain is tempting you to skip this question, you may want to thank it for sharing. Recognize that your brain is in fight, flight, or freeze. Acknowledge that this is new territory and tell your brain that it's safe to try this new way of thinking. If you truly want to live your life intentionally, please take a moment to answer this question.

In only three minutes, we can decide what we value the most—right now. This is the first step toward self-awareness and being on purpose.

You can decide what you value the most—right now.

With practice, it becomes easy and natural for you to ask yourself what is significant to you and others before you say or do anything. Give it a try and notice the powerful impact this has on the result that is achieved because you are focused, grounded, and proactive versus reactive. Notice the difference in what you do or say in a telephone conversation, at a meeting, in a memo, when you're making plans for an initiative at work, a vacation, and when you're having dinner with friends or family.

Noticing how you feel helps you determine if what you want is right for you or wrong.

In *Managing Thought* workshops, this is usually the time when I am asked questions such as, *What if I choose the wrong thing to want? How can I be sure that what I want is what serves my purpose? What if I think that what I want truly matters and it shouldn't?*

As we talked about in Chapter 5, noticing how you feel helps you determine if what you want is right for you or wrong. First, take a moment to quiet yourself and imagine that you are already living the life you want. What are you like in each moment of your day now that what you want is in place and working perfectly? What are you doing? How are you being? Say the answer out loud and in the first person. Always use the present tense, as if you are telling someone else your story. If you are feeling like a victim, being judgmental, or blaming others as you tell your story, chances are good that what you say you want is not right for you. It may instead be what other people want or what you think you *should* want.

An extremely powerful technique to determine if what you want is what truly matters to you is to take another step in self-awareness to discover the essence of what you want. I find it helpful to keep asking myself *What does this bring me?* or *If I could have it right now, would I take it?* until I get to the real answer—the essence of what I want. Then I am able to determine if the essence of what I want is true for me, whether it brings me peace or inspires me, whether it brings me toward the reality I want.

Now notice how you feel. Does the essence of what you want feel significant and of value to you? Does it bring you peace? Inspire you? Or does it make you feel bad? Do you feel a sense of inner power? Or do you feel forced or burdened by what you say you want? Do you feel like a victim? Are your eyebrows furrowed? Are your chest and neck tight? Is your breath short? If you do not feel at peace or inspired, then what you

If you do not feel at peace or inspired, then what you want is not from your higher awareness.

want is not from your higher awareness. These desires come from your lower awareness, and they are not want matters most *to you*.

Another Golf Lesson

Brendan wrote down seven words that defined what he considered to be a life well lived. He shared his words with his teenage daughter and was saddened when she criticized one of his words—golf. "Dad," she said, "that is so shallow."

He questioned if he was indeed shallow. He felt at peace and he felt inspired when he imagined playing golf as often as possible. He couldn't imagine not playing golf and was concerned about what he would do if he couldn't play golf. I asked Brendan to acknowledge the sadness he felt and to recognize that "golf" is true for him. I also asked him to get to the essence of golf—what did golf bring him? He discovered that the essence of golf was the opportunity to be with and enjoy the company of his brothers. He also felt an even deeper level of peace, knowing that if he wasn't able to golf anymore, he could still find many ways to enjoy and connect with his brothers.

> *You know you have reached the essence of what you want when you reach that which is permanent and can go no further.*

You know you have reached the essence of what you want when you reach that which is permanent and can go no further, when what you want is natural, not unnatural. Artificially created wants can never be fulfilled because they are not natural. Natural wants have their fulfillment contained within them, for they emerge from our center and are satisfied from our center. Unnatural intentions are imposed from without.

For example, years ago I wanted prosperity—a million dollars to be exact. I asked myself, *What does this bring me?* I answered, *Time to meditate. Time to go on walks. Time to read, study, and cultivate myself spiritually.* I asked again, *What does this bring me?* The answer was, *Balance.* My next question was, *What does balance bring me?* The answer was, *Balance brings me peace, joy, and enlightenment.* I learned that the essence of my want was peace, joy, and enlightenment, rather than prosperity. Peace, joy, and enlightenment are permanent, natural, and from within my higher awareness. *Time* and *one million dollars* are from without. It became clear that I didn't need time or money. I could start being true to myself and meditating, taking walks, reading, studying, cultivating myself, and living a balanced life.

A client of mine also wanted one million dollars. She believed that the million dollars would bring her security, which in turn would bring her the ability to retire early. She believed early retirement would bring her the ability to have fun, which in turn would bring her joy. In this process, she discovered that she did not need the million dollars to live a joyful life. She could start practicing experiencing the joy of each moment.

Another client overworked himself. He discovered that the overwork brought him perfection. Perfection brought him avoidance of failure. Avoidance of failure brought him a good reputation. A good reputation brought him good feelings about himself. Good feelings about himself

> *Ask yourself questions, quiet yourself, notice how you feel, and listen for the answer.*

brought him love for himself. Love for himself brought him peace. He discovered that overwork did not emerge from his higher awareness. He was looking outside of himself to find peace when peace could be found from within himself.

Another client absolutely hated her home. The main source of the disdain was that there was no fireplace. When she asked herself, *What does the fireplace bring me?* she discovered that what she really wanted was warm and special moments with her family. When she discovered what was true to her, she thought of several ways to create warm and special moments and to appreciate the special moments they were having every day.

The paradox? When I began to live a balanced life in each moment, and when my client focused on living moments of joy, we earned the million dollars. When the overworked man began finding peace in his moments, he began performing great work that earned him the great reputation. When the woman started enjoying her home, she received ideas on how to save money and within two years purchased her dream home with a beautiful fireplace.

Which *wants* emerge from your higher awareness? And which are imposed from without? How do you know? Self-awareness is the key. Ask yourself questions, quiet yourself, notice how you feel, and listen for the answer.

You know the answer. Please acknowledge and experience the joy of this self-awareness. Be thankful for your ability to discover the essence of what you want.

If you were to choose *just one thing* to practice from this book, it could be to start thinking about what you want and the essence of

Start thinking about the essence of what you want.

what you want. As you practice deciding what you want, notice how inspired and at peace you are because you are acting in accordance with what is true to you. You may also notice and become able to appreciate that you are already acting according to what is true to you.

Here is a short exercise to get you started—to help you understand what truly matters to you. This exercise can serve as the basis for practicing *Managing Thought* as you read the book.

PrioriTree I

What I Really Want

Determining What Is Significant and of Value to Me

_____

_____   _____

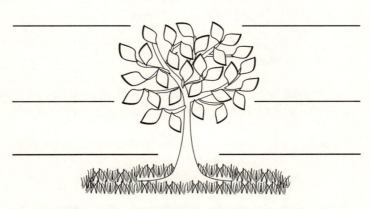

_____   _____

_____

1. Take a deep breath, first exhaling deeply to access your higher awareness.
2. Imagine that you are on your deathbed, congratulating yourself on a life well lived. Or think about an area of your work or life that is not working—where you may feel stuck.
3. Imagine what your life well lived is like. Or imagine what it could be like if you were unstuck—If what is stuck is working perfectly.
4. Write down seven words on the lines above to describe your life well lived or seven words that describe that area of your work or life as if it is working in the highest of ways.

(continued)

Examples:

For those who feel stuck in general or who are imagining a life well lived, words I have seen people write include:

Happiness, love, relationships, legacy, prosperity, peace, contribution, difference, security, family, abundance, joy, health, vitality, mentor, teacher, service, enlightenment, creativity, freedom, passion, purpose, balance, organized

For those concerned with being overweight, some of the words I have seen people write include:

Healthy, vitality, energetic, active, choices, vibrant, glowing, vacations, attractive, swimsuit, confidence

For those who are dissatisfied in their relationships with their significant others, some words I have seen people write include:

Loving, supportive, communication, trust, openness, romance, intimacy, accepting, embracing, partner, honeymoon, fun, comfort, sanctuary

For those who may be stuck at work, I have seen words such as:

Leader, respect, trust, openness, inspire, capable, execute, learning, satisfaction, growth, profitability, teamwork, fun, organized, planning, communication

5. **Now review your seven words and choose the word that is of most significance to you right now.**

6. **Circle the word.**

7. **Take a moment to reflect. What are you like in the moments of your day? Imagine what you want, not what you don't want.**

   For example, let's say that you are imagining being a great leader, a great partner, or a great parent, and your word is *listen*. As you imagine being a great listener, you may find yourself describing it in terms of what you don't want. For example, I don't let myself get distracted by all the things I have to do or I don't keep worrying about how I don't have time for this. As you catch yourself thinking about what you don't want, rephrase your story to describe what you do want. If you aren't distracted, what are you like? What do you think, do, and say? If you aren't worrying about the time, what are you thinking, doing, and saying?

Imagine each moment—I am a great listener. I take a deep breath, get into my calm space, and turn my attention to the person. I look into their eyes and smile. I am open and receptive to what they have to say. I ask questions to learn, and I repeat back to them what I have heard to gain a clear picture. I ask them how I can be of service to them.

8. **Write down seven words or phrases to describe what you are like at home, at work, and in life when you are living your word. What are you doing? How are you being? And what does this bring you?**

1. _____

2. _____

3. _____

4. _____

5. _____

6. _____

7. _____

9. **Take a moment to reflect. What did you notice?** Was this easy to do? Was it hard to do? Did you notice that

(continued)

thinking about what you want helps you to formulate a clear picture of the essence of what you want? If not, then branch out even further and write down seven words to describe your seven words until you have that clear picture of what it is like to live your word in the moments of your day. It is when you can imagine what you truly want that you become inspired. It is when you are inspired that you get ideas and take action to fulfill your intention.

10. **Tell your story. Say it out loud and notice how you feel.** To clarify your vision, test the power of what you think you want and to determine if it is true to you, say out loud, in the first person, what you have written in step 8 above. Say it in the present tense using full sentences, as if you are telling someone else about you. What do you notice? Does this feel inspiring? Does it feel good? Powerful?

If you feel blaming, judgmental, forced, or like a victim or do not feel at peace or inspired as you are saying your story, chances are good that what you are saying is not right for you. It may be what other people want or what you think you should want. Or perhaps you are focusing on what you don't want.

At this time, it is helpful to quiet yourself and notice the thoughts that come to you. You may have thoughts of how to change what you want or how to change the wording of what you want. In this case, go back and adjust what you have written, say it out loud again, notice, reflect, make adjustments again, and so on.

You may have thoughts of doubt, judgment, or that you *are* undeserving. In this instance, think about what you could prefer to think. Imagine what you are like when you think this way, say it out loud, notice how you feel, and make adjustments. Continue to peel your onion until you can describe how you are living that is true to your word and you feel powerful, at peace, and inspired.

This simple exercise can be used with anything we are about to do or say. We can write down seven words to describe what is of significance to us in being a parent, a partner, a teacher, a friend, a listener, a mentor, or a leader. We can write down seven words to describe what is of significance to us in a job, a career, parenthood, retirement, a vacation, a home, a relationship, or a marriage. We can write down seven words to describe what matters to us in a trade show, presentation, meeting, strategy, or goal.

> *With practice, we automatically think about what serves our purpose in each moment.*

With practice, before we say or do anything, we find ourselves quickly and naturally thinking about what is of significance to us in this moment. With practice, we automatically ask ourselves what we can say or do in this moment that truly serves our purpose.

In the next chapter, we take a next step in self-awareness and learn about thoughts that move us away from what we want.

*Only with self-awareness
can we begin
self-improvement.*

—Frank Moran

8

DESTRUCTIVE AND DISEASED THOUGHTS

When I have a thought that is not empowering or constructive for me or for the object of the thought, I let it go. If my thought is totally contrary to what I want (to what matters most for me and others), I let it go. How can we know whether a thought is destructive or diseased? These are a few rules of thumb that I use to help make that determination.

IDENTIFYING DESTRUCTIVE AND DISEASED THOUGHTS

Three Rules of Thumb

1. Does the thought bring me peace or inspire me?
2. Does the thought cause harm to others or to me?
3. Does the thought move me toward or away from what is significant and of value to me and to those involved?

1. Does the thought bring me peace or inspire me?

Thoughts such as worry, guilt, fear, anxiety, remorse, regret, sadness, disappointment, shame, anger, hatred, frustration, anxiety, jealousy, and being overwhelmed do not bring me peace. Nor do they inspire me.

If a thought does not bring me peace or inspire me, it is by its very nature destructive and diseased.

Thoughts of ill will, hatred, blame, judgment, criticism, self-doubt, unworthiness, and degradation do not bring me peace. Nor do they inspire me.

If a thought does not bring me peace or inspire me, it is by its very nature destructive and diseased. When I am thinking thoughts that do not bring me peace or inspire me, I am unable to access my higher awareness and creativity. I cannot think clearly or decisively. It is as if I am driving a car while looking through a dirty windshield.

When we are calm and at peace or inspired (yes, we can be calm and inspired at the same time), we make our best decisions. We know intuitively the next best step to take.

2. Does the thought cause harm to others or to me?

A thought could seem to bring me peace or inspire me yet wreak havoc on those around me. I think we can all agree that negative expectations and thoughts of ill will, hatred, blame, judgment, and criticism cause harm to others, particularly when we are in positions of influence.

Negative expectations and judgment cause harm to others.

Thoughts of self-doubt, self-criticism, unworthiness, degradation, limiting beliefs, and negative expectations that prevent me from achieving greatness, utilizing my talents, or taking the next best step are harmful to me. These thoughts also prevent me from being expansive, creative, abundant, true to myself, healthy, or happy and are therefore harmful to me. These thoughts are also harmful to others because when I limit my greatness, I am not of the highest and best service to others.

3. Does the thought move me toward or away from what is significant and of value to me and to those involved?

These are examples of thoughts that are contrary to the reality I want:

- I hate doing this.
- There's not enough time.
- It's difficult to change.
- I'm so out of shape.
- I just can't relax.
- All the good men are taken.
- The economy is causing our business to suffer.
- We can't find good people.
- My children (or my employees) are incapable of making good decisions.

These thoughts do not move me toward what is significant and of value to me. In fact, they move me away from it.

For example, if I want more time to spend with my family and I am constantly lamenting that I don't have enough time to do so, I am thinking a thought that is contrary to the reality I want. If I want to increase sales or cash flow and I am constantly worried about the lack of sales or cash flow, then I am thinking thoughts that are contrary to the reality I want.

Business executives often say to me, *Worrying about sales is what made me who I am today. If I didn't worry about sales, I*

Every thought we've ever had has made us who we are today.

---

wouldn't be motivated to do anything about sales. If you are thinking this way, I invite you to review your data. Look at all the actions and thoughts that you have had prior to becoming who you are today or prior to doing anything about sales.

The truth is that every thought we've ever had has made us who we are today. The questions are: Have we achieved our greatest potential? Are we living a happy, healthy life? Are we being of our highest and best service? I am reminded of a tree that is growing out of a crack in the pavement. Yes, the tree is growing, and considering the circumstances, it's doing well even to be alive. It is nowhere near the size and magnificence it could be if it were growing in its natural environment or under perfect conditions.

While the awareness of an initial worry thought (which is a fight, flight, or freeze thought) may indeed bring about the initia-

---

Our intentions to take action and the actions themselves bring about results.

---

tive to take action, it is not the worry thought that brings about the action. The intention to take action and the actions themselves bring about the improvement in sales. We choose to take action or not, or we choose to continue or succumb to additional worry thoughts. The additional worry thoughts do absolutely nothing toward the improvement in sales. They waste time, money, and energy. They lack clarity and focus and may actually move us away from timely, appropriate action.

In addition, worry thoughts, as with all thoughts of extreme emotion, negatively impact our health. Recent research shows that attitudes such as appreciation, care, and compassion significantly boost the body's immune system, whereas feelings such as anger, frustration, and irritation weaken the immune system. A 1998 study by the Institute of Heartmath showed that IgA (secretory immunoglobulin A), a key immune system component, was suppressed and well below normal for at least six hours after one five-minute episode of anger or frustration. IgA was boosted significantly after the research subjects focused on creating a sincere feeling of appreciation or care.

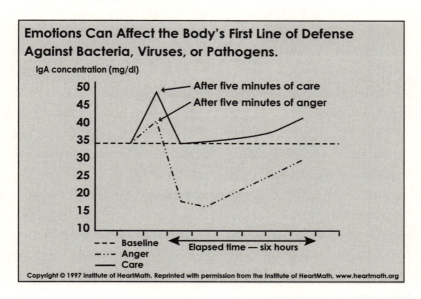

Emotions Can Affect the Body's First Line of Defense Against Bacteria, Viruses, or Pathogens.

IgA concentration (mg/dl)

After five minutes of care
After five minutes of anger

Baseline
Anger
Care

Elapsed time — six hours

Copyright © 1997 Institute of HeartMath. Reprinted with permission from the Institute of HeartMath. www.heartmath.org

Our bodies are chemical factories. They produce *good* and *bad* chemicals in response to how we choose to react emotionally to the circumstances and conditions of our lives. Each day, we have difficult people and experiences to deal with that can cause stress. How we manage our thoughts and emotions determines whether we continue to experience stress. We can choose thoughts and emotions that re-

> *We can choose thoughts and emotions that boost our immune systems and improve health and vitality.*

duce or eliminate stress. We can choose thoughts and emotions that boost our immune systems and improve health and vitality.

Researchers have also found that the hypothalamus is like a minifactory. It assembles certain chemicals that match certain emotions that we experience. For example, there are chemicals produced by anger, sadness, victimization, and lust. There are chemicals produced by every emotional state that we experience. And just as we can become addicted to heroin, we can become addicted to these emotion chemicals, psychologically and bio-chemically. We actually bring to ourselves situations that fulfill the biochemical craving of the cells of our body by creating situations that meet our chemical needs. An addict always needs a little bit more to get a rush or a high off what he or she is looking for chemically.

Often, we entertain thoughts that provide us with conflicting messages. We wonder which thought is really the constructive thought and which one is destructive. I find it helpful to repeatedly ask myself, *What does this bring me?* or *What happens or doesn't happen in my life when I attach to this thought?* until I get to the real answer—the essence of the thought. Then I can determine whether the answer is true to me. Does the essence of the thought bring me peace or inspire me? Does it bring me toward the reality I want or does it move me away?

When I was working late at night, I had two conflicting thoughts: one telling me to go home and the other telling me to keep working—to go the extra mile to be of service in my work. As my mission in life is being of service, it would appear that the thought telling me to go the extra mile to be of service was the true and constructive thought, and the thought telling me to go home was moving me away from what is important to me. I was surprised at what I learned when I kept asking, *What does this bring me?* of these two thoughts. When I asked, *What does "keep working to be of service" bring me?* I discovered that I had a need to be needed. This was a significant discovery. I had taken *being of service* to the extreme of *needing to be needed,* which was about me, not about servicing others. I could easily see that this thought did not bring me peace or inspire me. When I asked myself, *What does going home bring me?* I learned that rest and rejuvenation are significant to my being of highest and best service on a short- and long-term basis. This answer brought me peace and inspired me. Therefore, I knew that these thoughts were from my higher awareness.

A man in one of the *Managing Thought* workshops discovered that he had conflicting intentions. He intended *being driven* and *being calm and patient*. When he asked, *What does this bring me?* to each of these intentions, he discovered that his very definition of being driven gave rise to his conflict. To him, the essence of *being driven* was achieving results in a forceful way, yet he held the belief that calm and patient people are not driven. When he quieted himself, he healed his conflict. He realized that for him, being calm and patient while having a keen sense of purpose is what brings results.

Self-awareness is key. Ask yourself questions, wonder, quiet yourself, and listen for the answer. You know the answer. Please acknowledge and experience the joy of this self-awareness. Be thankful for your ability to choose your own thoughts.

When some individuals realize that they create their own reality, they become keenly aware of their counterproductive and even destructive thoughts. This

> *Keep asking,* **What does this bring me?** *to discover the essence of what you want.*

often leads to a fear of their negative thoughts. Many become afraid that if they have a negative thought or idea, they will create that reality. Thus they try to repress or ignore their negative thoughts and focus on the positive ones. This practice does not eliminate negative thoughts. Instead, another layer is added to the onion. It actually strengthens our attachment to the very thoughts we seek to eliminate.

You can relax. If you are conscious of negative thoughts, they do not cause a problem. When you are aware of what they are—just thoughts—you are observing the thoughts. You are not identifying with them. When you are aware of negative thoughts, realize that your negative thoughts are fight, flight, and freeze thoughts, and label them as such, they lose their power over you. They are well on their way out.

> *When you are aware of negative thoughts, they lose their power over you.*

We are told that it is the thoughts we hold *without awareness* and at *unconscious levels* that cause problems. This is why self-awareness is key. Because it is not that these thoughts are unconscious. It is that they are *not* conscious. Once we decide to start watching our thoughts, looking *at* them and not *from* them, the thoughts are there to be seen. Being curious about our thoughts, rather than judgmental, helps us be mindful. Being mindful of our thoughts, as well as our reactions and actions, brings about significant results, as opposed to the mediocre results we achieve when we live each moment *unconsciously* through force of habit.

> *Practice noticing whether or not a thought is serving your purpose.*

If you were to practice *just one thing* from this book, it could be to practice noticing what thoughts you have and deciding whether they are constructive for you or for others. Do they bring you peace? Do they create the reality you wish to create? Do they result in the character, circumstances, destiny, and success you want? Do they bring about what truly matters to you?

PrioriTree 2

Destructive and Diseased Thoughts

1. **Using the three rules of thumb for identifying destructive and diseased thoughts, take a few moments to review what you wrote in the Chapter 7 exercise PrioriTree 1—What I Really Want.**

2. **Think about the thoughts you have during the day.** What thoughts do you have that you know are destructive and diseased? What thoughts do you have that are not moving you toward the fulfillment of what is significant and of value to you? What thoughts do you have that are completely contrary to what you want?

3. **On the lines next to the dead and diseased branches above, write three predominant thoughts you have that you know are not constructive or empowering for you, perhaps even contrary to making what you have chosen as significant and of value to you a reality.**

4. **Look at these thoughts.** Without blame or judgment, notice how frequently you have these thoughts. Notice the impact

(continued)

these thoughts have on your creativity, passion, and zest for what you are doing. Notice the decisions you make and the actions you take as a result of these thoughts. Notice the impact on your health and the well-being of yourself and others.

5. **Can you think of any good reason to hold on to these thoughts? Can you think of thoughts that you prefer to hold on to, that could move you toward what is significant and of value to you?**

6. **Thank your brain for your thoughts.** Acknowledge and experience the joy of your self-awareness and your ability to choose your own thoughts.

*To understand
everything,
let go of
what you know.*

—Old Indian saying

9

THOUGHTS THAT WASTE TIME, ENERGY, AND MONEY AND BLOCK TRUE REALITY

In Chapter 8, we developed an awareness of thoughts that we know instinctively are not constructive for us and do nothing toward creating the reality we want for ourselves.

In this chapter, we develop an awareness of thoughts that we may not even realize are destructive. We are not aware of these destructive or diseased thoughts because we have a distorted or even a false view of reality. Imagine the sucker branches on a tree that steal the water, nutrients, and light. Destructive and diseased thoughts waste our time, energy, and money and block our light (our true reality).

An Exercise in Perception

Most of us trust that we accurately register the world around us. Isn't that what our brains do? The following exercise answers this question.

EXERCISE

Ask one or two people in the room with you to look around the room for about five seconds and identify everything in the room that is green. Then ask them to close their eyes. With their eyes closed, ask them to tell you everything in the room they saw that was blue.

When we do this exercise in *Managing Thought* workshops, everyone laughs. Very few individuals can identify blue items even if they were wearing blue or almost everything in the room is blue.

We laugh, yet it isn't a joke. It's an eye-opening and revealing truth for almost everyone. Because we are focusing on green, we do not notice blue.

Have you ever noticed that when you are making a decision to buy a car or have just gotten a new car, you suddenly see that same make and model of car everywhere? It's called the reticular activation system of the brain and it happens all the time. Our focus affects what we perceive.

In a famous study reported in the *Journal of Consciousness Studies*, subjects were asked to count the number of times two people portrayed in a video threw a ball back and forth. Most of the subjects were so intent on watching the throwing activity that they failed to see a black gorilla wander across the screen, stop in the middle, and beat his chest. What this study demonstrates is that our focus affects how we perceive things. And how we perceive in turn creates our reality.

As a result, we frequently make assumptions that are not true. We take things personally that have absolutely nothing to do with us. We then feel bad and make unworkable decisions—we say and do the *wrong* things and waste time, energy, and money.

Because we are often focused on the negatives, we miss the opportunities to experience the joy of our work, our life, and each moment. We also miss the opportunities to achieve greatness and make a significant difference.

In childhood, one of my favorite toys was a View-Master. With the press of a button I could view a series of pictures by inserting a slide wheel into the binocular-style viewer.

The way you perceive reality is like viewing the world through your View-Master. When you look at your surroundings and situations, interact in a conversation, write a memo or letter— as you experience each moment of your work and life—what slide do you have in your View-Master?

Is it a slide from your past? From your future? From your head? Your heart? Your gut? Your intuition? And in what order do you put your slides as you experience your life, your work, and your relationships? When I changed the slide in my View-Master and stopped expecting that certain people I worked with would be rude and unappreciative, and instead cultivated feelings of love, compassion, and appreciation for them, the dynamic of the relationships changed almost immediately.

> *Our expectations, beliefs, and past experiences affect how we perceive, which creates our reality.*

A Critical Lesson

Jim was excited because he had been working on changing his focus on what was wrong with his business partner to focus instead on what was right. It seemed to Jim that the relationship changed overnight. His partner began to voice appreciation for his talents and to bring up great ideas in a spirit of cooperation, instead of arguing and criticizing everything Jim suggested. Jim said that working with his partner became fun and that they forged a really great partnership because their skill sets were so different and complementary.

Jim was so pleased with this result that he decided to apply the technique to an employee issue. Jim began to change his focus on what was wrong with a problem employee and instead be thankful for the unique talents this employee brought to the company. Jim found that he was able to build on the employee's strengths and free him to be the best he could be. The employee, in turn, became willing and able to significantly change his management style.

Jim then decided to try this technique at home when he realized that he had an expectation that his wife should behave a certain way when he offered suggestions to her. He decided to release the expectation and discovered how loving and at peace he could be. He also discovered how happy and relaxed she became. Jim now swears by the power of perception in creating his reality. He now pays close attention to managing his thoughts and redirecting his focus to find workable thoughts and actions to achieve the reality he chooses.

Often, when I go into workshop situations, the coordinator of the workshop insists on telling me about each participant—*This gentleman is really close-minded, this one is rude and interrupts a lot, this one is argumentative*, etc. Understanding that this is a slide in the coordinator's View-Master, I do not put the slide in mine. Nor do I have a slide in which I expect anyone to behave in a certain way. To the amazement of the coordinator, the participant does not behave in the way the coordinator has come to expect.

Another example of the power of perception is the story about a study performed in the 1950s with teachers and students. In this study, a group that consisted of high- and low-performing students was divided into two classes, with each class comprised of an equal number of high- and low-performing students. The teacher was told that one class consisted only of high-performing students and the other consisted of only low-performing students. At the end of the year, the students were tested. Those in the high-performing class tested as high performing and those in the low-performing class tested as low performing.

When I shared this story at a *Managing Thought* workshop for the faculty of a school, a participant shared with me another story.

A School Lesson

At the outset of the school year, a teacher received her class list. As she reviewed the list, she was surprised to notice that a genius IQ was listed for each student. That school year, she invested much time and effort developing course outlines and special projects that her students would find interesting and challenging. At the end of the year, the principal paid her a visit and excitedly shared with her the test scores for her class. He said they scored extremely high and wanted to know what she did to achieve such great results. She shared with him that she went all out to develop course materials and special projects because they are geniuses. He stopped her and asked, "What do you mean, 'because they are geniuses?'" She replied, "The class list noted that they are geniuses." He looked at the class list and told the teacher, "These are their locker numbers."

I share these stories because they show vividly how we make decisions, take courses of action, and achieve certain results based on our beliefs and perceptions. These stories also demonstrate that our beliefs and perceptions affect not only our own reality. When we are in positions of influence, our beliefs and perceptions also affect the reality of others—for better or for worse. And we are in positions of influence many times each day with our partners, children, parents, colleagues, superiors, employees, customers, suppliers, and investors—everyone with whom we come into contact.

Again, it's a matter of self-awareness. It's about identifying the perceptions we have and deciding whether they are constructive for us or for others, bring us peace or inspire us, and create the reality we wish to create—the character, circumstances, destiny, and success we want.

When we understand and take responsibility for our own perceptions and understand that everyone's perceptions are different and have nothing to do with us, our world completely changes. We widen our view. We open ourselves to listen to others, to understand their per-

When we take responsibility for our own perceptions, our world completely changes.

ceptions, to love and accept others for who they are, and to love and accept ourselves for who we are.

Taking responsibility for our own perceptions—and seeking to understand the perceptions of others—produces significant results at work and in life.

We can now experience the joy of not having to be right. We can experience the peace and happiness of *maybe, I don't know,* and *I wonder.* We do not waste time, energy, or money taking things personally, being defensive, and getting upset over someone else's behavior. Gone are making excuses, judging, blaming, and criticizing ourselves and others. Instead, our heads are clear. We have access to our higher awareness and creativity. We are calm and available to sharply focus our time, energy, and money on learning, strategy, solutions, making a difference, and achieving greatness. We focus on what serves our purpose. We are also truly able to listen to others and be fully present as we interact with them. We ask clarifying questions as we seek to understand their perspectives.

The results gained from listening are highly significant for you and others—in many ways. I remember Susan Scott, author of

Fierce Conversations, saying, "Being listened to feels so much like being loved that we can't tell the difference." We all know how we feel when someone is really listening to us and asking questions. We feel respected and valued. We feel loved, accepted, validated, and cared for. All of these feelings somehow free us to be ourselves, achieve our highest potential, contribute, and make a difference—in other words, to soar.

And what about the thoughts you have about yourself? Do you listen to yourself? Do you ask yourself clarifying questions? Do you respect and value yourself? Do you help yourself to feel loved, accepted, and cared for by you? Do you free yourself to be yourself, to achieve your highest potential, to contribute, to make a difference, to soar?

At a conference for CEOs that I attended, led by Richard Boyatzis, author of *Primal Leadership*, he asked us to think of someone who had positively influenced us in our lives or careers. We wrote down in general terms how this person related to us in order to produce such a favorable impact. We were amazed to see that the 150 CEOs that participated in this exercise had identified similar attributes: *They listened to me. They encouraged me. They trusted me. They saw a vision of me that I could not see.*

We were then asked to recall someone who negatively impressed us, who we would never want to be like or work with again. Once more, we were amazed to have similar stories with common themes: *They didn't listen to me. They didn't value or appreciate me.*

According to Boyatzis, in an interaction, the left prefrontal cortex of the brain lights up when we experience encouragement and appreciation or feel wonder and possibility. It is dark when we experience defensive or depressing occurrences. This is critical. The prefrontal cortex of the brain is involved in making decisions and establishing priorities. It is the creative region of the brain.

Significantly, the creative region of the brains of both the giver and the receiver are affected, and the effect can last for days.

Which type of influence do you want to be? Do you want to bring out the best in people? Or the worst? Do you want to inspire them to accomplish what is significant to you and to them? Do you want to light up the creative regions of their brains? Or do you want them to avoid you at all costs, to withhold help and ideas, or worse—to have their spark extinguished?

Now that you know that everyone's perspective is different and has absolutely nothing to do with you, it becomes easy to notice the thoughts that are sucking away your energy and blocking your light (true reality). It becomes easy to practice *not* taking things personally, to question your assumptions, and to wonder what is possible. It becomes easy to be fully present in conversations and situations, to listen and to ask questions in order to deeply understand another's perspective. With time, these skills become easy to practice.

> *The ability to ask questions, in an effort to understand deeply, dramatically increases our performance at work and in life.*

This ability to ask questions, in an effort to understand deeply, dramatically increases our performance at work and in life.

- We develop solutions that suit a wide view, taking into account the thoughts, perspectives, and feelings of others. We build consensus, which produces significant results with our families, our colleagues, and the organizations we support.
- We determine what matters most to our family members, colleagues, team members, bosses, partners, employees, and customers. We match what we do best with what they value and appreciate. This results in the effective use of our time, energy, and money—and significant reward.

- We understand what inspires our children and those with whom we work. We then develop a culture and an environment that maximize their sense of being valued and appreciated, encourage their involvement, and drive their performance.
- We are able to understand what bothers others. We are then able to anticipate their needs and to think of potential solutions. In the marketplace, we are able to predict trends and innovate. This makes us effective.
- We develop and negotiate compromises in a cooperative way, with a commitment to win-win situations. We explore all options until mutually satisfactory solutions are reached.

All of these dramatic improvements are made possible through self-awareness—through understanding and taking responsibility for our own perceptions and beliefs, and through understanding that everyone's beliefs and perceptions are different and have nothing to do with us.

> *We change the world around us by changing ourselves.*

We achieve greatness as leaders, partners, followers, team players, parents, children, siblings, teachers, politicians, and so on.

We change the world around us by changing ourselves. When we change our thoughts, we change our world. We change our lives, our relationships, our circumstances, our performance, and our success. We achieve significant results by becoming aware of, taking responsibility for, and changing the thoughts that waste our time, energy, and money and block our light (true reality).

Beliefs

What we focus on affects how we perceive, and what we perceive creates our reality. Because of our focus, expectations, ingrained beliefs, lifetime of experiences, and the conclusions we have reached as we have lived our lives, we do not see the same reality of a situation. We each see our own perception of reality.

In this context, beliefs are significant. They are the seeds of our intentions, which, of course, are the seeds of our goals, strategies, and plans, which are the seeds of our reality.

> *Beliefs are the seeds of our intentions, which are the seeds of our reality.*

If we have mastered letting go of destructive and diseased thoughts, theoretically we have let go of the beliefs and expectations that are not constructive and limiting. Often, these beliefs are so deeply ingrained that we do not recognize them as being weak or nonconstructive. We

> *If we remain unaware of our limiting beliefs, they continue to rule our world.*

think of these beliefs and expectations as facts. We may even say that we are being realists when, in fact, we have a slide stuck in our View-Master. Negative and limiting beliefs are real trouble-makers when we are not aware of them. These detrimental beliefs are the deepest, most fundamental assumptions and expectations we may hold. We may have beliefs about life, the world, ourselves, and others that immobilize us or continue a cycle of struggle and undesirable results. As long as we remain unaware of these limiting beliefs, they continue to rule our world.

For example, I wanted prosperity. Yet each time I made significant sums of money, I lost it. Later, I discovered that I held a self-limiting belief that I could not be a wealthy person *and* be a spiritual person. I replaced that slide in my View-Master with a new slide: *I am of highest and best service and I am richly rewarded. My prosperity is a source of good for me and for others. My prosperity prospers others. I spend my money on causes that matter to me.* It was then that I began to build wealth.

Making Belief Work for Her

Emily believed that her life was out of balance. She worked during the day, and she also had four children for whom she cared. Her day was so full of responsibilities that she felt there weren't enough hours in the day to meet all of them. She practiced every possible time-management technique to no avail. As she learned about *Managing Thought,* she discovered that she had an underlying belief that if others did something for her, she was in their debt. Complicating this was another underlying belief that she never wanted to owe anybody for anything. As a result, she could not ask her family, her husband, her children, or her friends for help. She could not delegate or ask for help or advice from her boss or her colleagues.

When Emily realized that she could try on another belief, her life began to change for the better. She realized that she could be thankful for the contributions that others made to her success. With this new belief, it was easy for Emily to ask for help and enjoy the results. She also enjoyed expressing her appreciation for the help she received.

Addressing her underlying thoughts resulted in a transformation that could not occur when Emily merely tried to change her behavior or action. When Emily's thoughts became thoughts of thankfulness and purpose, she felt at peace and inspired. It was then that the ideas came to her on how she could live the word balance.

Our beliefs and expectations come in all different sizes, shapes, and colors. More often than not, they are destructive in the sense that they are weakening and limiting and keep us focused on what we don't want.

Here are some limiting beliefs that convince us of our inadequacies and shortcomings:

- I have a bad memory.
- I am a slow learner.
- I am no good at math.

- I don't have a degree.
- I have no credentials.
- I am too old.
- I am too young.
- I am a woman.
- I am a minority.
- I am overweight.
- I am unlucky.
- I never win anything.
- I have a bad temper.
- I am ugly.
- I am disorganized.
- I am a realist.
- I hate confrontation.
- I don't apply myself.
- I'm not disciplined.
- It's out of my control.
- I'm not good at anything.
- I'm not good enough.
- I am lazy.
- I'm not good at sales.
- Nobody likes me.
- I can't hold people accountable.
- I'm not cut out to be a leader.
- Nothing good ever happens to me.
- Nobody respects me.
- Nobody listens to me.
- Nobody cares about me.
- Nobody trusts me.
- Nobody supports me.
- There's nothing I can do.

These limiting beliefs convince us we shouldn't be, or can't be, successful:

- If I'm successful, I won't have time for myself or my family.
- If I'm successful, my friends and family won't accept me.
- To be successful, I have to be dishonest.
- To be successful, I have to be manipulative.
- To be successful, I have to be ingratiating.
- It is impossible to be successful in business and be a good person.
- To be successful, I have to think only about profit.
- To be successful, I have to have a degree.
- To be successful, I have to be younger (or older).
- I don't deserve to be successful.
- Success always eludes me.

We may have limiting beliefs about what it means to have power:

- Powerful people think only of themselves.
- Powerful people make other people feel inferior.
- Powerful people are dictatorial.
- Powerful people are forceful.
- Powerful people are aggressive.
- Powerful people are exploitative.
- Powerful people are demanding.
- Powerful people are destructive.
- Powerful people are inconsiderate.
- To become powerful, one has to step on other people.
- I am powerless.
- I have no power.
- There's nothing I can do.

We may have limiting beliefs about relationships:

- All the good ones are married.
- I don't have time to meet anyone.

- Men, they're all the same.
- Women, I'll never understand them.
- Men don't show emotions.
- Men don't do their share of the housework.
- Women want to talk all the time.
- Men are stoic and in control.
- Men should shoulder more of the financial burden.
- If he loved me, he would know when I need a hug.
- If she loved me, she would initiate sex more often.
- He doesn't tell me he loves me ___ times per day, so he must not love me.

We may have beliefs that make us feel superior to others and limit our ability to learn, be open to another perspective, improve, or achieve greatness:

- I am beautiful.
- I am handsome.
- I have a high IQ.
- I am smart.
- I am a quick learner.
- I have a degree.
- I am the boss.
- I am the president.
- I am in charge.
- I am the parent.
- I am the highest-ranking person.
- I am the head of the family/organization/committee.
- In my day, ___
- There's only one way to do things, and it's my way!
- They have no idea what it's like to ___
- They don't know what they're talking about.

- They're lucky to be doing business with us.
- They're lucky to have a job here.

We may have limiting beliefs that affect our ability to see the truth or the reality of a situation and result in our pain and suffering:

- He should be more competent.
- She should say thank you.
- She should take responsibility.
- They should be up-front with their opinions.
- I should spend more time with my family.
- I should exercise more.
- He, she, it, they should ___
- He, she, it, they shouldn't ___
- She should do her homework without my having to ask.
- If I am in pain, I must have done something wrong.

The following are limiting beliefs about life in general:

- Nothing is easy.
- Life is tough.
- Reality bites.
- No good deed goes unpunished.
- The world is a dangerous place.
- What can go wrong, will go wrong.
- Every day I fight the good fight.
- It's a man's world.
- It's a white man's world.
- No pain, no gain.
- Money doesn't grow on trees.
- Money is the root of all evil.
- It's tough to get ahead.
- There's not enough time in the day.

- Good things don't happen to good people.
- Bad things happen to good people.
- There's no such thing as a free lunch.
- I can't be happy until ___
- You can't teach an old dog new tricks.
- You never have a second chance to make a first impression.
- It's not what you know; it's who you know.
- There is a glass ceiling.
- If I am in pain, it's someone else's fault.
- If I suffer enough in this life, then I will be rewarded in the next.

Families may have their own collective, limiting beliefs:

- We all have a bad temper.
- We're firemen, or miners, or morticians. That's what we do.
- If you can't say something nice, don't say anything.
- If something goes wrong, it's someone else's fault.
- If something goes wrong, it's my fault.
- You must always do your best.
- God will provide.
- It's us against them.
- We always stick together.
- A women's place is in the home.
- Money will solve our problems.
- It's just one thing after another.
- Boys don't cry.
- It's against our religion.

Organizations also subscribe to limiting beliefs:

- It's impossible to find good people these days.
- Our people can't change.
- We just don't have enough time.
- Customers won't pay a higher price.

- We're different; what works for you won't work for us.
- Sales are always down in a bad economy.
- We can't attract the best people.
- We can't execute.
- To grow, we have to steal business from the competition.
- That's the way it's done in this industry.
- This is the way we always do it.
- If our organization is successful, we won't be flexible.
- If our organization is successful, we'll lose our *family* culture.
- If our organization is successful, we'll become bureaucratic.
- If our organization is successful, it won't be fun anymore.

Societies ascribe to limiting beliefs:

- We are separate and distinct from everyone else.
- Democracy is bad.
- Democracy is good.
- More is better.
- Less is better.
- Men and women are different.
- Men and women are not different.
- Capital punishment is good.
- Capital punishment is bad.

Specifically note the limiting beliefs of organizations that if we are successful, we won't be flexible, we'll lose our *family* culture, we'll become bureaucratic, and it won't be fun anymore. I often come across these limiting beliefs. One client of mine had a significant opportunity to grow. Yet his beliefs in the negative consequences of success held him and his company back. They ignored opportunities, sabotaged themselves, didn't put in place systems and processes that could help them win this new business, and neglected to hire people who could help them rise to a new level of capability. When the president recognized the limitation of his beliefs and decided what he wanted—being successful *and* flexible, keeping the family culture *and* having fun *without* being bureaucratic—he freed himself and his company to grow substantially.

At this moment, your brain might be saying to you that *I have a degree* isn't a belief—it's a fact. Thank your brain for sharing, and take another step in self-awareness. Notice the thoughts that follow (remember that thoughts come in groups). It is the thoughts that follow that may signal the limiting belief. For example, *I have a degree and I don't value the perspective of anyone who doesn't have a degree.* Or *I have a degree and I deserve an increase in pay because I now have a degree.*

As with perceptions, if we rely on our beliefs as true, we make decisions based on them. Our beliefs then become self-fulfilling.

A young business manager was telling me that it was time for him to hire people for his growing business. With sadness, he told me that he couldn't find good people in his area.

This thought is common: *We can't find good people.* Making this statement creates a self-ful-

> *If we rely on beliefs as true, we make decisions based on them, and our beliefs become self-fulfilling.*

filling prophecy. First, if our brain tells us that we can't find good people and we make decisions relying on this statement as being true, we close ourselves to the possibility that we *can* find good people. We become unable to access our higher awareness and creativity. When we close ourselves to possibility, we choose not even to bother to think about all the steps we could take to find good people. We choose *not* to gather information about our company, our culture, our mission, our future, our industry, our area, and so forth, which we could present to make ourselves attractive to good people.

We choose *not* to develop programs to attract the brightest students at the local high schools or colleges, which give them flexible hours and money to apply to tuition. We choose *not* to develop a recruitment program designed to search for the brightest and best.

Second, when we think that we can't find good people, we close ourselves to the possibility that the people we hire are good, or even great. We close ourselves to the possibility of greatness. We choose *not* to invest in orientation programs or the training of these new employees because we believe they weren't good in the first place. We choose *not* to ask for their input or make an effort to inspire them because why should we bother, since they aren't good anyway? We choose *not* to bother to raise the bar or set stretch goals because we think that we are limited in our ability to execute or to grow.

Third, because of the brain's reticular activation system, we don't even notice the greatness of each of our people because we have trained ourselves to notice only what is wrong. Then we perceive that they don't perform well and we say, *See! We can't find good people.* Then our brain stores yet another incident of, *We can't find good people,* which it then presents to us the next time we want to hire. Our very beliefs and expectations affect our intentions, strategies, goals, plans, decisions, and ultimately our actions, which then create our circumstances, reality, and results.

And let's not forget our belief in statistics. To me, statistics are nothing more than a reflection of mass belief systems. Lily Tomlin once said, "Reality is nothing but a collective hunch."

Until Roger Bannister shattered the four-minute-mile barrier in 1954, the feat was thought to be impossible. *It's flu season. Eighty percent of companies that reorganize under Chapter 11 don't make it.* These are also examples of mass beliefs that become self-fulfilling.

A Statistics Lesson

Jan owned a retail establishment and was gravely concerned about doing construction on the inside of her store. She had learned that the statistics in her industry showed that stores like hers lost 20 percent of revenues during the construction. She then believed that if she embarked on this construction project, her revenues would drop 20 percent. She was afraid of moving forward because, if her business dropped 20 percent, there wouldn't be enough money to survive. I asked Jan what she could do if she focused instead on what she wanted, for example, to increase her business by 20 percent. As she wondered about what she wanted, bringing about vision, purpose, and possibility, her face relaxed, and she became animated while speaking of her ideas to increase the business by 20 percent. Remembering the 80-20 Rule, Jan realized that while most businesses have decreased their revenues during construction, that didn't have to be true for her. Without blame, judgment, or being a victim, she looked at what she could do to prevent a decrease, and she looked at what she could do to increase business. She found herself inspired. The fear vanished, and she knew what to do. Jan decided to move forward. Rather than letting a belief in statistics rule her world, she implemented the ideas and her business increased by much more than 20 percent.

The following story illustrates how beliefs affect the decisions we make, and the actions we choose to take, and dramatically affect results.

A Lesson in Results

Volunteers were staffing phones at a local television station, answering questions from viewers. Before they started, they had gone over the script and the leader emphasized that when they were finished answering the callers' questions, they should ask the callers if they had heard about their organization, and get their names and e-mail addresses so the volunteers could send them their information.

(continued)

One of the volunteers said that he didn't think callers would give them their names and e-mail addresses because so many people are concerned about being on a list that then gets sold. Another volunteer agreed. The leader assured them that they do not sell their list, and that they could assure the callers of that fact as well. At the end of the two-hour session, the volunteers each had collected fifteen to twenty names, except for the two volunteers who believed that most people would not want to give their information. Each of them collected only two names.

Dr. Norman Vincent Peale, a champion of positive thinking, once told an interviewer the story of a man who was told by his doctor that he had an incurable cancer. Mentally devastated, the man went home and proceeded to deteriorate in health. He was near death when his doctor discovered that he had made an error and had looked at the test results of another patient. In fact, he did not have cancer at all. He should have been a picture of health, yet he was near death from believing that he had an incurable cancer.

When I questioned my belief that troubled company situations bring out the worst in people, I noticed many people behaving in an upstanding way. When I changed my belief that I couldn't be successful in business *and* be a good person, I began to meet many successful businesspeople who were great people, and I began to recognize my own goodness and success. When I changed my belief that lessons in life have to be learned the hard way, I began to learn my lessons in a joyful way. When I changed my belief that a challenge has to be painful and difficult, I began to experience fun and exciting challenges. When I changed my belief that there isn't enough time in the day, I found I have plenty of time to do what truly matters to me.

It is critical to take an inventory of our perceptions and beliefs because they are the seeds of our intentions.

It is critical to take an inventory of our perceptions and beliefs because they are the seeds of our intentions, which of course, are the seeds of our goals, strategies, and plans, which are the seeds of our reality, our experiences, and our results. This is true for us as individuals. It is also true for families and organizations.

I remember learning about the Denison Organizational Culture Survey ten years ago as a member of TEC/Vistage. They shared with our group of CEOs the premise that the culture of an organization dramatically affects business performance. At the time, the concept was fairly new, and I remember many of the executives thinking that it was hogwash, saying, *You can't tell me that soft stuff affects results.*

Today, after twenty years of research on over 1,500 organizations, the Denison Organizational Culture Survey reports that the culture of an organization indeed has a significant impact on the organization's performance in areas such as profitability, quality, sales growth, innovation, and customer and employee satisfaction. In fact, the survey has shown that organizations with a great culture earn a return on equity of 21 percent versus a return on equity of only 6 percent for organizations with a low-performing culture. This is a huge difference.

What is significant to me is their definition of culture: *The underlying beliefs, values, and assumptions held by members of an organization, and the practices and behaviors that exemplify and reinforce them.* They define beliefs and assumptions as *the*

> **Beliefs and assumptions drive results.**

underlying, unwritten, taken-for-granted beliefs, perceptions, thoughts, and feelings that are the ultimate source of values that guide employee behavior.

Beliefs and assumptions drive the culture of an organization, an individual, and families. Beliefs and assumptions drive performance. They drive results.

As you identify a perspective or belief that you hold, sit with it without judgment. See, feel, and notice it with gentleness and compassion. Then ask yourself, *What does this belief bring me?* listen for your answer, and notice how you feel. Notice if your belief contributes to achieving your purpose. Do you feel the belief is helping or hindering? Do you feel encouraged or discouraged? Does it increase your power or diminish it? If the belief is not powerful for you, if it does not serve your purpose, then it's time to try on a new belief.

> *Deeply recognizing a limiting belief may be all that is needed to dissolve it.*

Can we change our belief systems overnight? Sometimes we can. Experience has shown me that deeply recognizing a limiting belief may be all that is needed to dissolve it.

Using techniques to shape your thoughts completes the dissolution. It may take a few days, sometimes a few weeks, months, or years. I find that the beliefs held by organizations are easier to identify than personal beliefs. Sometimes it is helpful to have a partner or a professional assist us in identifying our beliefs. In the next chapter, we learn how to uncover limiting beliefs.

*When the doors of perception
are cleansed,
man will see things
as they truly are,
infinite.*

—William Blake

10

DISCOVERING AND RELEASING LIMITING PERCEPTIONS AND BELIEFS

In Chapters 8 and 9, we developed an awareness of thoughts that are destructive and diseased and negatively affect our view of reality. We learned that beliefs may be so deeply ingrained that we may not even realize that they are beliefs. We believe that they are reality. As I mentioned earlier, deeply recognizing a limiting belief is sometimes all that is needed to dissolve it, and so in this chapter we learn how to uncover and release limiting beliefs.

There are a few rules of thumb that I use to help identify and release limiting beliefs.

DISCOVERING LIMITING BELIEFS

Nine Rules of Thumb

1. Be sensitive to how others react to what you are saying or doing.
2. Pay attention to how you feel and what you feel most strongly about or most right about.
3. Watch for absolutes—statements with extreme words.
4. Watch your *But*!
5. Turn *You* into *I*.
6. Pay attention to the nonconstructive beliefs of others and ask yourself if you hold those beliefs.
7. Get to the heart of the matter.
8. Notice the story you tell about yourself.
9. List potential roadblocks and obstacles to achieving what is significant and of value to you and notice any thoughts that signal underlying limiting beliefs.

1. Be sensitive to how others react to what you are saying or doing.

Others may look at you incredulously. They may roll their eyes or stare blankly. They may express frustration or exasperation, saying things like, *Why would you think that? Where is that coming from? How could you possibly say that?*

As we read in Chapter 8, when we are open to and appreciate the perspectives of others, we realize that their perceptions are different and have nothing to do with us. There is no need to take their reactions personally. We can practice being open and receptive to learning about what they are thinking and feeling. We don't need to get defensive or upset over their perceptions or behavior. Instead, we can practice asking them questions—delving deeply, seeking to understand, learning their perspectives, and perhaps trying on a new belief.

2. Pay attention to how you feel and what you feel most strongly or most right about.

When we are fused with a thought, it shows up in our bodies. When we feel threatened or under attack, that is usually a sign of a belief at work.

The very nature of a belief is limiting if it prevents us from being open to possibilities.

When we feel right and strongly about something, that feeling is usually rooted in a belief, which may or may not be limiting. The very nature of the belief is limiting if it prevents us from being open to the infinite sea of possibilities, the alternative ways to see, do, or experience things. The belief is limiting if it prevents us from moving in the direction of what serves our purpose. Again, we don't need to get defensive or upset over the perceptions or behavior of others. We don't need to prove that we are right or make someone else a loser. Instead, we can ask questions, seek to understand, gain a new perspective, and try on a new belief.

If in this process you discover that you have a need to be right, the steps in *self-awareness* discussed in Chapter 7 may be helpful to you. Try asking yourself, *What does being right bring me?* until you discover the essence of what you want. Perhaps it's feeling important which brings the respect of others, self-respect, and self-love. Or perhaps it's expedience, which brings temporary results. Only you know your answer. Once you discover it, you can begin to define and shape your thoughts in the moments of your day to align with what you really want. For example, if you discover that results are what you want, you might choose seven words to define what excellent results mean to you. You might discover that the development of others is what serves your purpose. You might then discover that sharing your experiences with others instead of telling them what to do helps them develop their own skills to handle what comes their way. In this case, you might prefer to practice thinking, *What experience or story can I share to help others develop their own expertise?*

3. Watch for absolutes—statements with extreme words.

Watch for words, in your thoughts and in your speech, that are extreme in nature. Words such as *can't, won't, always, never, no way, must, should, have to, has to, it's always been this way, everybody, and all* finalize your decision and close the door to the wide range of possibilities.

Our brains may be telling us:

I can't do it. It can't be done.

There's no way. It is always this way.

It will never happen.

Everybody is like this.

They all do it this way.

There's no way we can make it.

I should do this.

I have to do this.

It has to happen this way.

If we believe that we are our brains, it is impossible for us to see, or to look for, other possible ways of being. In essence, we have already decided that there is no other way, and as a result, we do not look for or see any other alternatives.

In addition, cutting off possibility extinguishes our creativity and sense of play. Have you been in a meeting or in a situation where an idea is offered and someone immediately says, *It can't be done?* Did you notice the effect on the participants? The enthusiasm dissipates. If you find yourself using

> **Cutting off possibility extinguishes our creativity and sense of play.**

such a statement, stop and ask yourself, *If this were possible, what could I do? If there was a way, what could it be?* or wonder what is possible. As you ask these questions or invoke the state of wonder, feel the changes in you. Notice yourself feeling a sense of freedom, as if you have released yourself from a self-imposed prison. Notice how you feel uplifted and inspired. Allow yourself to feel the creative portion of your brain light up as your creative juices begin to flow.

Many people are familiar with the story of Walmart. What they may not realize is that Walmart achieved its initial success by questioning the conventional wisdom—or belief—of the retail marketing world.

Walmart examined the belief commonly held by retailers that relied on a narrow formula of revenue numbers per square feet of floor space. Instead, Walmart focused on service, on what was important to its customers—a sense of community, a place to sit and rest while walking around the big store. Walmart also questioned the long-held belief of retailers that it is necessary to stock inventory. By asking, *If we didn't stock inventory, what could we do?* Walmart revolutionized the retail industry.

4. Watch your *but.*

The word *but* in a sentence may serve as a signal of a limiting belief of hopelessness or insufficiency or a belief that it is not possible for two thoughts to coexist or that two thoughts have to coexist. As an example, a friend of mine told me that his goal for the year was to reduce his debt, *but* he couldn't collect on a big receiv-

> ### The word but *may serve as a signal of a limiting belief.*

able. He seemed sad and hopeless as he stated his goal. His *but* ties the two thoughts together, when in fact they are two different thoughts that can be dealt with separately. His *but* does not bring him peace, nor does it inspire him. His creativity on debt reduction and on receivable collection is squelched. When he separated the two, he could feel the difference. He felt a sense of freedom and felt a sense of wonder and possibility that he could reduce his debt whether or not he collected the receivable. He could develop separate intentions and a course of action to reduce the debt and to collect the receivable. His hopelessness transformed into inspiration.

Another man told me that he tried to keep a good attitude, *but* there are lots of people with bad attitudes with whom he deals every day. He had a sense of quiet desperation—a feeling of hopelessness that no matter how good his attitude, there would always be people with bad attitudes. I asked him to replace the word *but* with the word *and.* When he said, "I do my best to keep a good attitude, *and* there are lots of people with bad attitudes that I deal with every day," he lightened up and felt a sense of relief. He recognized that he can do his best no matter how others behaved. He was free to feel good about doing his best, no matter what others did.

At a leadership conference I recently attended, the keynote speaker commented that when working on new company initiatives, leaders want differing opinions among their people when they are conceptualizing new initiatives and developing plans, *but* they want consensus when they execute. She went on to say that most of us lean toward consensus when we are developing our plans, which is ineffective.

I wondered what the reason is that most of us lean toward consensus when we are developing our plans, even though this is ineffective? It is because we have the limiting belief that we can't have differing opinions in the planning stages *and* consensus in execution. Yet these two realities *can* coexist. If we instead believe that we want differing opinions in conceptualizing new initiatives *and* we want consensus in execution, we can be very effective. Intel has a very powerful philosophy: "Disagree and commit." Notice the word *and*.

> *We learn quickly and effectively when we're in a state of joy and thankfulness.*

I often hear the word *but* in meetings. For example, *We had great numbers for the first quarter,* but *we have lots of work to do to meet our numbers for the year.* The word *but* completely discounts the joy, inspiration, and power that come from the recognition of a job well done for the first quarter. The *but* focuses instead on what *has to be done,* which, as we learned in Chapter 5, is not powerful. It makes the rest of the year feel burdensome, and creativity is squelched. It's a downer. *We had great numbers for the first quarter* and *we have lots of work to do to meet our numbers for the year* has a very different feel and brings about very different results. *We had great numbers for the first quarter,* and *by focusing on ___, we achieve our numbers for the year* is even better. *By focusing on ___, we achieved ___ and had great numbers for the quarter and by focusing on ___, we achieve our numbers for the year* produces an even greater impact because we are keeping our vision and purpose top of mind. Remember, we learn quickly and effectively and are inspired and creative when we're in a state of joy, thankfulness, vision, purpose, wonder, and possibility.

I exercised today, but *I ate a lot of things that were bad for me.* This statement takes away the joy and power of the acknowledgment of progress made in exercising today and keeps me focused on what I don't want, for example, eating foods that are bad for me. *I exercised today* and *I ate a lot of foods that were bad for me.* This statement helps me acknowledge the exercise and observe the eating choices I made. *I exercised today* and *I ate several cookies and drank soft drinks.* This statement brings about even better results because it acknowledges the eating choices without judgment. *I exercised today* and *I ate a healthy breakfast.* This way of thinking produces even greater results because the focus is on what I did right, which is the reality I want.

I acknowledge and celebrate the good choices and forward movement. I am now free to look forward to learning about and making good choices tomorrow.

Watch your thoughts and speech, and notice how many times you use the word *but*. Practice immediately replacing it with the word *and* or with a period, separating the thoughts into two sentences. Notice how much better you feel and how

> *Practice replacing **but** with **and**. Notice how much better you feel.*

responsible you feel for your own happiness and well-being. Or if you like, when you catch yourself using the word *but*, check your data. What are the facts? Are the two parts of the sentence directly causal? Most of the time, the sentences are not directly related. Rephrase the sentence, either separating them completely or changing the word *but* to *and*. Then notice how much better you feel.

Change *I just landed this new job,* but *I don't know if I can handle it,* to *I just landed this new job*, and *I don't know if I can handle it.* Feel the difference. Change it again to *I just landed this new job*, and *I wonder if I can handle it.* Change it again to *I just landed this new job*, and *I wonder how to handle it.* Change it again to *I just landed a new job*, and *I'm curious how I can contribute to the company's success.*

The word changes are subtle yet impactful. Notice the difference in how you feel. The change of words brings back a state of wonder, curiosity, and possibility. It lights the creative part of your brain. It lights your soul. If you say it with a smile and with your eyes wide open, as if you were a child imagining the possibilities and trusting that it will work out great—that it *is* working out great—you'll feel an even greater impact.

5. Turn *you* into *I.*

The use of the word *you* when you are explaining your situation or your feelings to others signals the limiting belief that your situation or feelings are universal and not your own—that this is the way it is for everybody. It's not. It is only what is true for you. Using the word *you* gives away your personal accountability and responsibility for your circumstances, your feelings, and your life. The following sentences are some examples:

> Well, it's so busy at work *you* just don't have time to take a breath. *You* just can't get everything done. *You* go home at night and *you're* exhausted.

> *You* just can't find good people these days.

> *You* just can't get ahead in this situation. *You* try and try and *you* get so frustrated.

> *You* know how it is when *you* have a new job. *You* have to start over again, and *you* have to prove yourself. *You're* meeting so many people, *you* just can't keep them straight.

> John, a CEO, said to me, "It's hard when *you* merge. *You* have two different groups of employees coming together and *you've* got two different cultures. It's hard when *you* try to change a culture."

By saying *you*, John is saying that he believes that it's hard for *everyone* to merge, that it's hard for *everyone* to bring two cultures together and to change a culture—that this is reality. Since John believes that it's hard for everyone, he also believes that he is justified in having a difficult merger and in feeling bad. The likelihood of John lighting the creative region of his brain, looking for and developing ways to make merging two cultures effective and fun, enjoying the merger, and inspiring his people is quite slim.

What if John, instead, had said the following sentence? *Well, this merger is hard for* me. I *have two different groups of employees coming together and* I *have two different cultures. It's hard for* me to *change a culture.* John immediately takes ownership of the situation and realizes that he is responsible for his world. By saying *I* and *me*, he takes personal responsibility for the merger and the culture and then asks himself if this is what he wants. Does he want this to be difficult? Does he want to feel down about how hard this is going to be? Does he want to be the one responsible for the difficulty in merging two cultures? No. Because he is expansive by nature, he begins to wonder what could be done differently to merge and change cultures. He begins to ask questions—to learn and develop courses of action. He inspires others to do the same.

Here's another example:

MARY: How's your diet coming?
DAVE: *You* know how it is when *you're* on a diet. *You* try to eat small portions, but it just tastes so good, *you* can't stop.

By saying *you*, Dave has not taken responsibility for his own thoughts, feelings, and behavior. He is assuming that this is how it is for everyone, *and* it's normal

Although something may be common, that does not mean it is normal, natural, or true for you.

for him to be feeling this way. Dave said to me, "This *is* how it is for most people." I responded, "While something may be common, it does not mean that it is normal or natural. It does not mean that it is true for you." Remember the 80-20 Rule. It may be true for 80 percent. It does not have to be true for you.

If Dave says, I *try to eat small portions and it tastes so good*, I *just can't stop*, Dave begins to take responsibility for his choices and his behavior. He progresses another step up the ladder of self-awareness and mastery. He is now in a position to ask himself what he truly wants and reshape his thoughts to create his desired results.

> Mary: What's happening with your son?
> Susan: *You* know how teenagers are. And when *you're* a
> parent, *you* worry that *you're* doing the right thing. *You*
> want to set boundaries, yet *you* don't want to alienate
> *your* child.

By saying, *you*, Susan is saying that all teenagers are alike. Her relationship and all of her interactions with her son are exactly like everyone else's. She feels bad and lacks confidence.

By saying, *I worry that I am doing the right thing. I want to set boundaries and maintain a good relationship with my son*, Susan

> *Replacing the word* you *with* I *brings about significant transformation and results.*

takes responsibility for and ownership of her relationship with her son. She then begins to wonder how she could set boundaries *and* maintain a good relationship. She begins to seek advice on the best course of action. She begins to choose her intentions and ask questions that lead her to the reality she intends.

Instead of *You can't find good people*, say *I can't find good people*. Feel the difference. Change *You go home at night and you just don't have any energy* to *I go home at night and I just don't have any energy.* Instead of *You can't forgive yourself,* try *I can't forgive myself.* Notice what it is like to take personal accountability for a world you do not want. Notice how you begin to wonder what you can do to change your world.

If you were to implement *just one thing* from this book, replacing *you* with *I* can have a dramatic impact on your ability to achieve significant results. For me, changing *you* to *I* brought about significant transformations in every area of my life. In less than a year I witnessed

> *Notice what happens when you take personal accountability for your world.*

profound changes in my personal life and professional life. When I took responsibility for my beliefs, beliefs that didn't fit with the way I wanted to live and be, I wanted to shake them off right away as if they were old, wet dirty clothes. I wanted to try on new beliefs—put new slides in my View-Master. I became aware of my world, and I took responsibility for it. I changed the world around me by changing myself.

6. Pay attention to the nonconstructive beliefs of others and ask yourself if you hold those beliefs.

It can be helpful to learn from others' experiences and discoveries. In Chapter 9, I listed sample beliefs for this purpose. These beliefs surfaced frequently in workshops and in social settings. The list is by no means exhaustive.

During a meeting, one CEO was telling another that it's hard to find a good controller. The second CEO thought to himself, *That's odd; finding good controllers hasn't been difficult for me. Finding good salespeople—now, that's hard.* The lightbulb went on when he realized that he had been saying to himself that it's hard to find good salespeople. He changed his belief and hired great candidates in less than two weeks.

7. Get to the heart of the matter.

We often have beliefs that mask our truth. For example, we may find ourselves thinking, *Our customers don't appreciate us.* If we want our customers to appreciate us, this belief is focused on what we *don't* want. It squelches vision, purpose, wonder, and possibility. We are forever stuck in this reality until we can discover the real truth to this belief.

We often find ourselves bothered, even angered, by certain behavior and situations centered on a certain theme. For instance, if you made a list of what really bothers or angers you, you may notice a theme. The theme might be respect, integrity, or appreciation, for example. There are at least three possibilities of the truth of your anger. One possibility is that these are qualities that you want to improve in yourself. Through the reticular activation system, you notice this in others and it's easier to be bothered by others than by yourself. If this is the truth, it's best to thank your brain for the observation and move on.

Another possibility is that these are qualities that you do not exhibit toward yourself. Due to your reticular activation system, you are focused on how others treat you the same way. If this is your truth, it's best to thank your brain for the discovery and practice treating yourself the way you want to be treated.

When actions of others bother you, restate your belief to seek the truth of what you are feeling.

Another possibility is that this is your gift—a value that you hold dear and by which you live. Perhaps you do show respect, you do appreciate others, you do have integrity. Realizing that this is your gift and that others do not have the same gifts can help dissipate your anger and give you cause to appreciate yourself and remain committed to your gifts.

Whenever the thoughts and actions of others bother you, restate your belief (out loud if you can) in order to seek the truth (essence) of what you are feeling. First, restate your belief as if you have this belief about others: *We don't appreciate our customers.* Restate it again as if you have the belief about yourself: *We don't appreciate ourselves.* Then restate it yet again, as if this is your gift: *Appreciating others is our gift. It is what we do well.* Notice how you feel as you make these restatements. Which thought rings true or truer? For example, change *They don't respect me* to *I don't respect them*, and then change it to *I don't respect myself.* Now change it again to *Respecting others is my gift* and see which thought rings true or truer.

When we discover the truth, we are free to practice thoughts that are aligned with what we want. We may choose seven words to define what showing appreciation looks like and then practice thinking along those lines during the moments in which we interact with our customers. Or we may choose seven words to define how we might show appreciation to ourselves and institute these practices. Or we might choose to acknowledge that appreciation is our gift and ask how we can serve as an example to others.

There are times when we believe that people *should* behave or situations *should* happen in a certain way, and we are bothered, even angered, when they do not. We have a set of rules by which we live, and we think that somehow the whole world has the same set of rules. Darned if they aren't always breaking the rules, and darned if we aren't always bothered by it.

Albert Einstein defined insanity as doing the same thing over and over again, expecting a different result. If we keep getting bothered by thinking, *He* should *be more responsible,* and he's not

Once you have discovered your truth, you are free to access your higher awareness and create solutions that move in the direction of what you want.

responsible and never has been, then who's insane? Who doesn't have the grip on reality? I find that many people are frustrated because whatever they are working on isn't going smoothly or as planned. For some reason, many people expect that the line between point A and point B is always going to be perfectly straight. The truth is that there are usually curves, and even a few backward motions.

When you catch yourself thinking *should,* change *should* to *is* or *could* and see what happens. Or practice thinking, *I notice that I am having a thought that this* should *happen.* Now distance yourself from that thought and notice how you feel. You may discover that you are being judgmental. Or you may discover that you are attached to one outcome. Once you have discovered your truth, you are free to access your higher awareness and create solutions that move in the direction you want. Often, it's best to put a new slide in your View-Master, accept what is, and then wonder which direction is best for you to fulfill your purpose. Then notice what happens.

Getting to the heart of the matter is a significant step in self-awareness and in releasing limiting beliefs.

8. Notice the story you tell about yourself.

We all have a story that we tell others and ourselves, a way we define and describe our lives and ourselves. The story is just that, a story. The story can be fact or, more likely, fiction. Our story is really a listing of beliefs—some of these beliefs can be working for us, and some, against. A question you may want to ask yourself is, *Whose beliefs are they?* Are they yours? Your parents'? Or are they the beliefs of your teachers? Colleagues? Friends? Society? Perhaps they are the beliefs of the media? I do not believe it's necessary to ask ourselves where a belief came from. The appropriate questions are, *Are these beliefs true to me?* and *Are these beliefs working for me?*

Self-awareness is key when it comes to deciding whether a belief is constructive for you. A belief may be constructive for a friend of yours and not for you. A belief may be constructive for you in one situation, yet not in another. A belief may be constructive for you today and not

> *Self-awareness is key when it comes to deciding whether a belief is constructive for you.*

tomorrow. Only you, through self-awareness, know the answer to whether a belief is moving you toward or away from the reality you want.

Ole Carlson, in *Beneath the Armor: How Business Leaders Stand Tall in a Turbulent Global Economy,* talks about changing his story. He recalls how, as a nine-year-old, he was shipped off with his eleven-year-old sister to distant relatives he didn't know. He found it necessary to adopt a story—or mental strategy—by which he perceived himself as autonomous and independent. The story worked well enough for the boy to earn scholarships for his academic achievements and later to succeed in the world of business. Nevertheless, as the years passed, the autonomy and independence stories that had served him so well began to be perceived as aloofness and arrogance by his professional colleagues. He realized that the story wasn't working for this mature stage of his life, so he changed it. He changed the autonomy and independence story to an intimacy story—appropriate and effective in his current situation.

"Bless your old story," writes Carlson, "because it was a trusted comrade, who proved tremendously valuable in transporting you to where you currently are. If no longer appropriate, put it to rest. An appropriate and respectful eulogy is in store. With arms and heart wide open, welcome the new version of your story. You are simply accessing another part of yourself. It was there all along."

Often, people tell the same story, usually a sad one, again and again: *This happened when I was a teenager, and now I'm like this.* Or *This happened to our business, and now we're like this.* There are three techniques you can use to release these limiting beliefs.

The first technique is to make up three to five stories explaining the reasons you are the way you are today. You'll find that the more stories you make up, the less fused you become with your own.

A second technique is to pretend that you have three chairs— the sad chair, the happy chair, and the inspirational chair. Then retell your story while sitting in each chair, relaying only sad information in your sad chair, happy information in your happy chair, and what you learned and how you grew in your inspirational chair. As you do this, you are removing the sad story slide from your View-Master and replacing it with a new slide.

A third technique is to separate the two parts of your story and then check your data. For example, separate *This happened when I was a teenager* and *I am like this.* Then look at all of the experiences you have had and the choices you have made that contributed to your being the person you are today. You then see the many separate experiences and choices you have made that have influenced you. You may discover that you have had a series of slides stuck in your View-Master all along.

You can change the slides in your View-Master. You can change your stories.

9. List potential roadblocks and obstacles to achieving what is significant and of value to you and notice any thoughts that signal underlying limiting beliefs.

I have found it incredibly useful to list the potential obstacles and roadblocks to the reality I want. I quiet myself and listen to the thoughts in my head telling me what the real obstacle is—the real essence of the obstacle—the limiting belief that lies deep within. A client of mine wanted balance. She listed all the obstacles, which included inadequate staffing, emergencies of clients that required her immediate attention, a difficult business partner, etc. When she quieted herself and reviewed the list, she discovered the underlying belief that she had a need to be the savior—the one who rode in on a chariot to save the day. She discovered her belief that she didn't deserve to be happy, that it wasn't possible for her to achieve her personal financial goals with this business, and that she could not achieve balance until she achieved these personal financial goals.

Once you have identified these underlying limiting beliefs, take a moment to wonder what you could prefer to believe. Rewrite the belief to reflect the reality you intend. For example, my friend rewrote her limiting beliefs as follows: *I am inspired by the work I do. I provide great service to the company. I am happy. I deserve happiness. I am balanced. I can do this.* She repeated the new beliefs out loud to test them and noticed how she felt. She

Rewrite your beliefs to reflect the reality you intend.

continued to make adjustments until she discovered beliefs that were true to her and inspired her.

A colleague of mine listed two phrases representing what is of significance to him in leading a successful life: being *loving* and being *focused*. As he listed the obstacles, the thoughts that came to him revealed a circle of beliefs that made it impossible for him to fulfill his intentions of being loving *and* being focused: *It is hard for me to focus. If I am focused, I will put tasks before people. Putting tasks before people is not loving. If I say no to people in order to remain focused, I am not loving.* He rewrote these beliefs as follows: *I focus easily and effortlessly on what truly matters. I am of highest and best service to others and to myself. I am loving.* He also began to wonder how he could say no to others and be loving. Ideas then came to him about how to respond to those who requested his time and money, and now he responds with a sincere thank you and referrals of resources that may be helpful.

> *We do not need to know where a limiting belief came from to let it go.*

I am often asked about the importance of understanding what caused a limiting belief. Many have said to me that they *have* to know where the belief came from in order to let it go. (This in and of itself is a limiting belief.) I do not feel it is necessary to understand where the belief came from. I find that when we remain focused on what is significant now, the cause of the limiting belief eventually rises to the surface and presents itself to us to be released. During a quiet time, we may recall incidents that gave rise to the belief. Or we may suddenly find the belief triggered by a similar event. If we are observing our thoughts, we can see the belief thought and remember the cause.

If we are trying to find the cause of a belief, we are distracted from what actually *is* in this moment. We are focused on what is going on in the rearview mirror. If we are trying to find the cause of a belief because we *need* to validate who we are today, we are focused on judgment and criticism of who we believe ourselves to be. We are distracted from who we truly are. And what happens if we stop our lives to find out the cause of a belief? What does the answer actually give us? Does the answer help us choose which direction we want to go now?

As an example, when companies and individuals encounter a difficulty, the tendency is to focus on who did something wrong. This tendency usually brings about blame, judgment, and criticism. These thoughts extinguish joy, gratitude, learning, and creativity. If instead the focus is on vision and possibility, that which is wrong either dissipates or safely rises to the surface to be seen.

Let's take a few moments to become aware of the beliefs and perceptions we may have that are holding us back from fulfilling what is important to ourselves and to all involved.

Although you may be tempted to skip over this exercise, I invite you to take these few minutes to expand your self-awareness. You will be glad you did. Your beliefs have consequences, for better or worse. They are the seeds of your intentions. So it's good to take inventory—to notice and acknowledge your beliefs without blame or judgment. This diminishes their power and releases them.

> *The power of a belief is diminished when you observe your belief without blame and judgment.*

Again, this is a matter of self-awareness. It's about noticing the beliefs and perceptions we have and deciding whether they are constructive for us or for others, whether they bring us peace or inspire us, whether they create the reality we wish to create—the character, the circumstances, the destiny, and the success we want.

Taking responsibility for our beliefs is key because every detail of the belief system that we hold has consequences—for better or for worse. Simply bringing the awareness of some of these underlying beliefs to light causes some of them to dissipate immediately. For others, it is necessary to make a conscious effort to shape thought, which is the subject of the next chapter.

PrioriTree 3

Thoughts That Waste Time, Energy, and Money and Block the Light (True Reality)

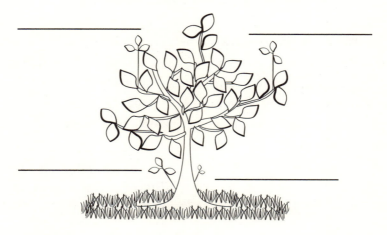

1. **Write down the word that represents what Is significant and of value to you from Chapter 7.**

2. **As you write your word and Imagine what this word represents as being reality, notice the thoughts that come to you that are telling you how or why this reality may not be possible or why It may be difficult. Write the limiting beliefs on the lines next to the suckers and crossed branches on PrioriTree 3 above.**

3. **Based on what you learned in Chapters 8 and 9, and in this chapter, write additional predominant thoughts you have that you know are perceptions, beliefs, expectations, or conclusions drawn from prior experiences that are wasting your time, energy, and money, and are contrary to making what is significant and of value to you a reality.**

Examples:

- Thoughts that you are right about something.
- Thoughts that you feel strongly about something.
- Thoughts that limit possibilities—can't, won't, must, no way, it'll never, should, always.
- Limiting beliefs—beliefs about inadequacy, success, power, superiority, or life in general; from an individual, family, organizational, or societal perspective. (You may want to review the lists of limiting beliefs in Chapter 9 to see if any of these ring true or trigger you in any way.)
- Thoughts where you expect things to happen or people to behave in a certain way.
- Criticism, blame, or judgment of yourself and others.
- Conclusions you've drawn from prior experiences that are no longer valid today.

4. **Look at these thoughts**. Without blame or judgment, notice how frequently you have these thoughts. Notice the impact these thoughts have on your creativity, passion, and zest for what you are doing. Notice the decisions you make and the actions you take as a result of these thoughts. Notice the impact on your health and the well-being of yourself and others as a result of these thoughts.

5. **Can you think of any good reason to hold on to these thoughts?**

6. **Acknowledge and experience the joy of your self-awareness and your ability to choose your thoughts.**

As with perceptions, our beliefs shape our lives and the lives of others, particularly when we are in positions of influence. The following story illustrates how our beliefs have an impact on the lives of others—for better or worse.

Our beliefs have consequences—for better or worse.

An In-Law Lesson

Jerry, a CEO, shared with me that he and his wife deeply believed that their son-in-law was not the right man for their daughter. He didn't have a high-paying job, he didn't have a degree, and he seemed unambitious. Their interactions with their son-in-law were not friendly, and they exhibited no interest in him, or he in them. Needless to say, they, their daughter, and her husband were not at peace or inspired when they were in each other's company. When Jerry and his wife became aware of the slide in their View-Master, they decided to replace the slide with the belief that their son-in-law was, indeed, the right man for their daughter. They began treating him with respect, expressing an interest in his life and beliefs, and genuinely caring about him. In a short while they noticed a change in their relationship with him. He began talking to them more, sharing his hopes and dreams. He began asking questions about going back to school and possible careers. He began working and went back to school. It was an *aha!* for Jerry and his wife to see that by changing their belief that their son-in-law was a loser, holding instead a higher vision, and treating him with care and respect, they freed their son-in law to be himself and be the best he could be.

When we understand and take responsibility for our own belief systems and understand that everyone's beliefs are different and have nothing to do with us, we can widen our view. We can open ourselves to listen to others, seek to understand their beliefs, and love and accept them for who they are. Moreover, we can widen our view with respect to ourselves. We can open ourselves to listen to our own inner guidance and to love and accept ourselves for who we are.

We achieve greatness as leaders, partners, followers, team players, parents, children, siblings, teachers, and politicians. We change the world around us by changing ourselves. By changing our thoughts, we change our world, our lives, our relationships, our circumstances, our performance, and our success. We achieve significant results.

BEING ON PURPOSE

Happiness is when what we think, what we say, and what we do are in harmony.

—Mahatma Gandhi

All we achieve
and all that we fail to achieve
is the direct result
of our own thoughts.
You are today
where your thoughts have brought you;
you will be tomorrow
where your thoughts take you.

—James Allen

11

HOW TO SHAPE THOUGHT

In the previous three chapters, we developed our self-aware-ness—noticing the thoughts that are not constructive and prevent us from achieving the results we want for ourselves, our families, and our organiza-tions. In this chapter, we look at being on purpose and focusing our thoughts, actions, reactions, time, money, and energy on what is of value. When we are on purpose, we know what matters to us and we make the most of every moment. We are focused on moving in the direction of our purpose, in service of what deeply matters to us. We overcome the 80-20 Rule in work and in life.

When we are on purpose, we know what matters to us and we make the most of every moment.

At this point, you are no doubt aware of thoughts that are not in service of your purpose. You may find yourself thinking that you *really need to get rid of* these negative thoughts. You may notice that a significant portion of your sixty thousand daily thoughts are thoughts *about* your thoughts—thoughts analyzing or defending the original thought. You may even be afraid of your negative, counterproductive, and destructive thoughts because you do not

want to create that reality. You
may find yourself focusing on
your negative thoughts. You
may find yourself arguing with

Focusing on your negative
thoughts produces more
negative thoughts.

these thoughts or trying to repress negative thoughts in order to
focus on what you consider to be positive rather than acknowledging what is without blame or judgment. Feeling that you *should*
or *need* to get rid of a negative thought does not get rid of it. To
the contrary, the focus on your negative thoughts produces more
negative thoughts, as we learned earlier in this book. The
need to focus on identifying negative thinking adds even more
layers to your onion. Do not fall into this trap. Replacing weak
thinking with weak thinking that is disguised as powerful
thinking is not the answer. Thank your brain for sharing and
gently extricate yourself from these thoughts of judgment, criticism, worry, and fear.

Relax and know that when we are consciously aware of negative
thoughts, they do not cause problems. We are aware of what they
are—thoughts—and we do not identify with them. When we are
aware of them as thoughts, they lose their power over us. They are
well on their way to being cleared out or dealt with quickly and
effectively.

The thoughts we hold without conscious awareness are those
that cause problems. This is why self-awareness is key. Being
mindful of our thoughts, actions, and reactions brings about
significant results, versus the mediocre results we achieve by living
each moment *unconsciously*, through force of habit.

Furthermore, there is far more power in focusing on the
powerful thoughts we want to have versus the negative thoughts
we don't want to have. David R. Hawkins, MD, Ph.D., in his
book *Power vs. Force*, demonstrates that the power of a thought
can be measured. He has determined that "the difference in

Focusing on powerful thoughts counterbalances many of the weak ones.

power between a loving thought (10–35 million megawatts) and a fearful thought (10–750 million microwatts) is so enormous it is beyond the capacity of the human imagination to easily comprehend."

What this tells me is that just a few powerful, constructive thoughts a day can counterbalance all of the weak, nonconstructive, and fearful thoughts we have. We can be far more effective in work and life, and in transforming our thinking and our realities, by focusing on the powerful thoughts we want to have, not the weak thoughts we don't want to have.

How Do I Let Go of a Thought?

The key to success in letting go is in the *letting go*. See the thought for what it is—a thought—and don't let it rule your world. There is no need to attach to it. There is no need to identify with it. We can practice looking *at* the thought, not *from* the thought. The key is self-awareness—it takes self-awareness to notice the thought. It takes self-awareness to decide whether the thought is constructive and in service of my purpose. It takes self-awareness to observe that there isn't any good reason to to look out at the world from the thought. And it takes self-awareness to do all this without judgment, blame, or criticism. There is no need to judge, blame, or criticize my brain for doing its job.

One powerful technique to separate ourselves from our thoughts is to name the thoughts. For example, you might say to yourself, *Oh—there go my worry thoughts*, or *there go my fear thoughts,* or *there go my sad story thoughts,* or *there go our it's-a-bad economy thoughts.* You will find that just by acknowledging and then naming the thoughts, they become less powerful. They can be seen for what they are—thoughts that you can choose to have or let go, thoughts that you can choose to look *at* or look *from*. Eknath Easwaran, founder of the Blue Mountain Center for Meditation, simply says, "Out!" to a thought he does not want.

Another technique is to distance yourself from the thought. For example, once you observe the thought *I am worried about sales,* add the thought *I am having the thought that I am worried about sales* and then the thought *I notice I am having the thought that I am worried about sales.* Finally, add *I notice my brain is presenting me with the thought that I am worried about sales.* Creating distance helps remind us that we are not our thoughts and we are not our brains. Saying to your brain, *Thanks for sharing—I'll take it from here,* also reminds us that we are not our thoughts.

> **See a thought for what it is— ust a thought.**

You may be more of a visual person, in which case you can picture the thoughts disappearing. One creative man told me that he pictures a thought in a cloud above his head, just as if it was a thought balloon in a comic strip. Then he imagines the balloon and the thought being zapped away. One woman told me that she pictures her thoughts going out a revolving door. Another woman told me that she imagines thoughts floating away down a river in a canoe. Another man told me that he pictures putting his thoughts into an envelope and dropping it into a mailbox.

Clearing your head and calming yourself are additional techniques to use to let go of negative thoughts. You may choose to exhale and inhale deeply until the thoughts have cleared (see Chapter 18). Alternatively, you may choose to take a drink of water, go for a walk, work out, play, dance, listen to certain music, or remind yourself of your intention.

Instead of letting go of a thought, we may want to reword it to transform it to a powerful thought. In Chapter 5, we learned that if we don't feel at peace or inspired as we think a thought, there is another way to think the thought to serve our purpose. For example, we may discover that changing a *you* to an *I*, a *but* to an *and*, a *should* to a *could*, or a *need to* or *have to* to a *choose* is all that is needed to transform a thought. Or perhaps we can change a forceful thought to wonder or bring a future thought to the present to transform that thought to serve our purpose.

Can you notice a destructive or diseased thought and learn to let go of or transform it overnight? If you can, that's great. Often, simply bringing the awareness of a thought and the recognition that the thought serves no useful purpose can cause the thought to dissipate immediately.

Recognizing that a thought serves no purpose can cause it to dissipate.

Other times, it is necessary to make a conscious effort to shape your thoughts—to practice thinking the thoughts you choose to have.

How Can We Shape Thought?

Our thoughts and thought patterns are habits and may be difficult to break. Our brains are very practiced and very fast. Again, the first step is self-awareness—observing the thought without blame or judgment. The second step is choosing your next thought. Less than one second before you hold a thought, you decide to hold that thought. Do you choose to let the thought go, transform it, or replace it with a new thought you have decided to practice? Or do you decide to continue thinking the thought and let it rule your world? When we are not self-aware, we allow our brains to go unsupervised, and they choose the thoughts we hold. We continue to go about our work and lives *unconsciously*.

Science has shown that as we think certain thoughts, certain neurons fire together and then wire together in a complex neural net, creating *the habit*. Science also has shown that neurons that stop firing together stop wiring together, so it's possible for each of us to reinvent ourselves and our lives. Although you may not be able to change your thoughts overnight, you can begin to pay attention and be mindful of your thoughts. You can practice noticing unconstructive thoughts and letting go of those that do not serve you, or you can practice replacing them with thoughts that do serve you. Experience and your practice of noticing and adjusting your thoughts create new neural nets and new habits.

The way we feel and what we experience come from what we focus our attention on at any given moment. If we are focused on green, we see and experience green and not blue. If we are focused on the ball, we do not see or experience the gorilla. We then make decisions, take actions, and pro-

> *By shaping our thoughts, we choose the direction and focus of our minds.*

duce a reality around the green or the ball. Our brains are constantly evaluating what we focus on in every moment. By shaping our thoughts, we choose the direction and focus of our minds. We achieve significant results.

I have learned that my brain is eager to answer questions and bring me information. It's like having a faithful dog that is only too happy to please me. I ask questions and make statements, and my *faithful-dog brain* brings back answers and observations that agree with me so that I am telling the truth. We are all about telling the truth. As we learned in Chapter 9, without self-awareness, what I think is true may not be reality or may not be what is really true to me.

So when my *faithful-dog brain* brings back information, I may make decisions and take actions that are not based in reality. These actions are not effective in the long run, and do not achieve the results I truly desire. If instead I shape my thoughts, my *faithful-dog brain* brings back answers and observations and I make decisions and take actions that are constructive. These actions build on the good to achieve greatness and are focused on what truly matters to me.

WE SHAPE OUR THOUGHTS BY:

1. Choosing our intentions
2. Asking ourselves powerful questions
3. Making powerful statements to ourselves
4. Replacing weak thought patterns with powerful thought patterns

---

As you begin to practice shaping your thoughts, you can develop your own tool kits. You may develop different tool kits for the different types of thoughts. For example, you may have a set of powerful statements ready for when you begin to experience self-doubt and another set for when you are angry. You may have a different set of powerful questions ready for different people; for example, coworkers, customers, or family members.

We learn how to shape thought in the following chapters.

*Go confidently
in the direction
of your dreams.*

*Live the life
you've imagined.*

—**Henry David Thoreau**

12

CHOOSING MY INTENTIONS

Our wants and desires are the seeds of our intentions, which in turn are the seeds of our strategies, goals, and plans, which are the seeds of our actions, our results, and ultimately, our reality.

To turn a desire into reality requires intention.

As we discussed in Chapter 7, to achieve what we want, we must know what we want, which can be difficult to discover. To turn what we want into reality requires more than just want and desire. For example, we may think about what we want and believe that it can never happen: *I want to be rich, I want a bigger house, I want to be respected, I want our company to be the leader in the industry.*

To turn a desire into reality requires intention. Intention is the spark that ignites the flame of desire and burns it into reality. Today's intentions become tomorrow's reality.

How Do We Choose Our Intentions?

- Do you have a written vision statement or intention for your organization or your family?
- Do you have a written vision statement or intention for your role in your organization or family?
- Do you have a written vision statement or intention for yourself? For your life? For your career?
- Do you have a written vision statement or intention for your relationship with your children? Your direct reports?
- Do you have a written vision statement or intention for your relationships with your customers, your suppliers, your investors, your employees, your colleagues, your manager or boss?
- Do you have a written vision statement or intention for your marriage, your education, your livelihood, your sustenance, your well-being, your success?
- Do you have a written vision statement or intention for your vacation, the home or car you want to buy, a conversation, an activity, a sales call, an acquisition, or a meeting?

We can set vision statements and choose our intentions and our purpose for any aspect of our being. You can *intend*:

- Good health
- Being a loving partner to your spouse
- Being a guide and mentor to your children or your direct reports
- Helping your employees fulfill their dreams
- Being of highest and best service to your customers, employees, investors, suppliers, children, parents, and humanity
- Being open, receptive, and kind in a conversation and using the interaction as a source of learning about yourself and others

And then, before you say or do anything, ask yourself what you can do in this moment that is consistent with your intention. Before you make a phone call or respond to a comment, before you join a meeting or have a conversation, before you open the door when you come home from work, exhale and inhale deeply. Remind yourself of your intention and ask yourself or wonder what you can think or do that moves you another step toward making your intention a reality.

With practice, breathing deeply becomes natural for you. With practice, reminding yourself of your intention and asking yourself how you can think and behave in a manner that is consistent with your intention also becomes natural for you. With practice, you are able to think these powerful thoughts just as quickly and naturally as your old thoughts.

> *Exhale and inhale deeply. Remind yourself of your intention.*

When we choose our intentions and are mindful, we achieve clarity of purpose. We are clear on what matters most to us, on what we value. When we are clear on our intention, how we react to a colleague, customer, family member, employee, or situation is very different from how we react when we are not clear.

For example, a man may have as his intention, *I enjoy and nurture the love between my wife and myself.* One busy day he is advised that his wife called while he was out. She sounded upset and asked that he call home as soon as possible. Before he picks up the phone, he takes a breath, brings to mind his intention, and adds to it, *I am so glad that my wife is at home and deals with things when I can't, and I am glad I can be here for her now.* How he relates to his wife and how he feels during the phone call are quite different from what they would be if he had rushed to return the call, *unconsciously* remained in fight,

> *Being mindful of our intentions focuses our thoughts on what is truly significant to us.*

flight, or freeze, and reacted to the stress. By choosing his intention, he empowered himself to be calm, loving, and supportive.

Being continually mindful of our intentions focuses our thoughts, strategies, goals, plans, actions, and reactions on what is truly significant to us. This is how we achieve significant results. This is how we transform our relationships, our families, and our organizations. We are focused on vision and purpose, we become inspired, and we are empowered to live the lives we intend.

A client called me for advice on a proposal to make to a new customer. The problem had kept him up at night the entire weekend. He told me that a potential customer had phoned him asking for certain drawings. These drawings were actually taken from my client by a former customer and not paid for. The potential customer was having trouble getting the drawings from the former customer, who finally had referred the potential customer to my client.

I could hear anger in my client's voice and said, "You seem so angry." He responded, "I'm angry that my former customer took the drawings, didn't pay, and now they have the audacity to send someone to us for the drawings." I asked him what this has to do with the new customer. "Nothing," he said, realizing he had a slide stuck in his View-Master. "What's your intention for working with a new customer?" I asked him. He then realized that he had lost sight of his intention to treat potential customers as potential partners. "Thanks, Mary," he said. "What did that take? Five minutes? And I wasted a weekend worrying!"

That was more than just a weekend. He lost sleep. He wasn't attentive to his family. He missed out on the joy of his family. He missed out on rejuvenating and accessing his creativity and higher awareness. How many of us have wasted weeks, months, years, or money because we didn't stop and take a moment to see if what we were thinking or doing was consistent with our intention—with what truly matters for us?

My client had several things going on in this one little incident. First, he was angry all weekend (destructive, diseased thoughts).

We shape our thoughts by choosing our intentions.

Second, he was focused on the problem with the old customer and didn't notice he had a new customer (blocking his light). Third, he had forgotten his intention for his life and his customers (shaping his thoughts and focusing on what is of value).

What we feel and what we experience depend on what we choose to focus on. We can control the direction and focus of our minds by shaping our thoughts. We can shape our thoughts by choosing our intentions.

To maximize the power of intention, there are nine rules of thumb I use.

SHAPING THOUGHT: CREATING YOUR INTENTION

Nine Rules of Thumb

1. Frame your intention powerfully.
2. State your intention in its highest way.
3. Frame your intention in the active, present tense.
4. Focus your intention on *being* rather than *doing*.
5. State the good that results as you live your intention.
6. Allow yourself to imagine your intended reality with as many of your senses and emotions as possible.
7. Write your intention down.
8. Read your intention out loud, notice how you feel, and make adjustments to your intention.
9. Think, state, and write your intention as often as possible.

1. Frame your intention powerfully.

Stating what you don't want does not define what you do want. Even worse, stating what you don't want creates the intention of what you do not want. It keeps you focused on exactly what you do not want, which creates the perception and reality of what you do not want.

It is my intention not to be inadequate or *I am no longer inadequate* produces a reality of being inadequate. Using the very words that represent what we don't want focuses us on what we don't want, in this case, being inadequate. Similarly, we do not want to state intentions such as *I intend being cancer-free* or *pain-free* or *debt-free* or *stress-free.* As we learned in Chapter 9, if we are focused on green, we see green and not blue. If we are focused on the ball, we do not see the gorilla. If we are focused on *cancer, pain, debt,* or *stress, we do not see or experience perfect health, vitality, financial well-being,* or *balance.*

In addition, when we are focused on what we don't want, we shut down our creativity and our ability to learn and learn effectively. We feel bad. When we state our intention powerfully, we feel inspired and creative.

State what you do want. If your intention is *I am calm and I don't let anything bother me,* you will continue to notice and focus on what bothers you and will not notice when you are calm. You will not build upon being calm. If your intention is *We provide value-added service, so we're no longer a commodity,* you will continue to focus on being a commodity, which is not the reality you want. Instead, try shortening the intention to *I am calm* or *We provide value-added service* and see how that feels. You may want to add details that are focused on what you want, for example: *I am calm. When I find myself in fight, flight, or freeze, I take a moment to add light. I exhale deeply and, on the inhale, I think to myself,* How can I help? *I notice my answers and act accordingly. Every ninety minutes, I take a moment to exhale and inhale deeply at least three times. When I find myself worrying, I exhale deeply and on the inhale I think to myself,* I choose peace.

2. State your intention in its highest way.

If, for example, the thought you wish to reshape is the limiting belief *I am inadequate,* your new intention need not be *I am adequate.* Instead, think about

---

Express your intention in its ideal and greatest state.

---

what you really want in its highest way. Do you want to be *great? Fabulous? Confident? The best? Inspiring?* What do you really want? If, for example, you don't want your product or service to be a commodity, what *do* you want? *To be a partner? A trusted advisor? Someone who provides great service for which you are richly rewarded?*

Professional basketball shooting coach Dave Hopla tells his students that the difference between being a good shooter and a great shooter is not to intend *making each shot.* He teaches his students to intend *swooshing each shot.*

Decide what you want and express your intention in its ideal state, in its highest, greatest way. Use your own style. Let's say you don't want to feel inadequate anymore in your work. You might write your intention as follows:

I am great at work. I know my strengths and the skills I bring, and I am open to learning every day. I clearly see the impact I have on the success of the organization and my colleagues. I am confident about my performance, and my confidence builds every day.

3. Frame your intention in the active, present tense.

Frame your intention as if it has already happened or is happening now. You are putting a new slide in your View-Master. Your brain now reacts, causing behavior and producing chemicals, as if your intention is true. When you state your intention in the present tense, you create your first *now* moment of vision and purpose.

A man in one of my *Managing Thought* workshops developed the intention *I will enjoy the time I spend with my children.* The *I will* part of his statement reminds me of a sign I saw in a British pub that said, "Free Beer Tomorrow." The next day the sign still said, "Free Beer Tomorrow." When

> *When you state your intention in the present tense, you create your first* now *moment.*

will there ever be free beer? When we use words such as *I will, I plan, I am going to,* and *I am able to,* we are creating a reality that keeps what we want in the future. We never get the free beer. Mission statements, communications with customers and potential customers, and policies and procedures of businesses are often stated in the future tense. As we learned in Chapter 5, these future thoughts are not powerful.

After we discussed this, he reformulated his intention in the present to say, *I am enjoying the time I spend with my children.* This is better, although the *I am enjoying* part of his statement is said as if he were an observer watching himself enjoy something instead of really experiencing and feeling the enjoyment. As we learned in Chapter 5, *I enjoy* brings about more power than *I am enjoying.* (Feel free to take a moment to close your eyes, say these statements out loud, and feel the difference.)

When the same man changed his intention to *I enjoy the time I spend with my children,* he could feel the difference. Others could feel the difference, too, and saw a change in his demeanor. His eyes lit up, he smiled, and his posture straightened. He was inspired.

At this point, you might say to yourself, *I enjoy the time I spend with my children, except when I don't!* If you feel this way, you might try instead to focus on your values and commitment—on your purpose: *I am a committed father. I value my role as Dad. I choose being present for my children.*

Often, it's a matter of providing more detail so that you can more easily imagine how you can live the intention in the moments of your day. Here's an example: *I enjoy the time I spend with my children. I take a moment and clear my head and give them my full attention. I watch them laugh. I listen to them giggle. I let go and I play with them. I offer them hugs when they need them. I ask questions and help them find their answers. I love giving them the space and freedom to share their thoughts with me. I am thankful for the time I have with my children.*

Providing more detail is particularly effective in business situations. When we can easily imagine how we can live our mission statement in the moments of our day, we become inspired and able to experience our mission *now*.

Try adding more detail to your intention and see what happens. Do these thoughts move you in the direction of what matters to you?

4. Focus your intention on *being* rather than *doing*.

This is the real essence of why it is effective and powerful to frame our intention as if we are experiencing it and feeling it. I have found that many aspects of the word *do* in our language create burden and anxiety. I have found the word *do* to be an extreme word that can carry with it a sense of force—a sense of demand or requirement, as in *I must* do *this or else.* I have found that the word *do* can carry with it a sense of blame and judgment—mostly for ourselves, because we haven't been doing whatever it is we think we are supposed to be doing. Force, blame, judgment, burden, and anxiety are not states of joy and thankfulness. Our creativity, happiness, and ability to learn and grow are squelched.

One gentleman developed the intention *I will do what it takes to be a great leader.* His body and face were tense and tight as he made the statement. He reformulated his statement in the present tense to say, *I am* doing *what it takes to be a great leader.* He said he felt okay as he said this. He tried again: *I do what it takes to be a great leader.*

This felt better to him, although not great. Then he changed his statement from doing to being: *I am a great leader.* This felt even better. He changed his statement again to remove the word *great,* which brought about thoughts of judgment, and focused on the essence of what he wanted: *I am a leader.*

When he repeated this new statement aloud, he could feel the difference. *I* am *a leader* felt much more powerful than *I do what it takes to be a great leader.* Others could feel the difference, too, and saw a marked change in his demeanor. His eyes lit up, he smiled, his posture straightened. He looked like a leader.

Again, you might say, *Well . . . I am a leader, except when I'm not.* If you are feeling this way, you can choose a thought that focuses on your purpose, such as *I choose leadership.* Or you might provide more detail so that you can fully envision how you are living the word *leader* throughout the moments of your day.

As we learned in Chapter 5, *I choose leadership* is a powerful thought and may feel more powerful than *I am a leader* when you are having trouble letting go of thoughts that you don't believe you can be a leader or you are critical because you believe that you aren't a leader or have not been a leader in the past.

If the thoughts ruling your world are *I have absolutely no idea how to become a leader,* take a breath and invoke the state of wonder: *I wonder how I can be a leader,* or *I wonder what I can do in this moment that is leadership.*

5. State the good that results as you live your intention.

Stating your intention in its highest way also involves aligning your intention with the good that results from this new way of being—including in your intention how you can be of service to others and to yourself as you are living your intention. Your intention is powerful, and likely to become reality when you are clear about what good results from the fulfillment of your intention.

You might add to the intention above: *I am great at work. I know my strengths and the skills I bring, and I am open to learning every day. I clearly see the impact I have on the success of the organization and my colleagues. I am confident about my performance, and my confidence builds every day. I help others enjoy their day. I help others do a great job and be the best they can be. I notice and appreciate the contributions of others to my success. I compliment them and thank them.*

> **You can create an intention of being of highest and best service and being richly rewarded.**

I have found that there are many who hold back their potential because they feel guilty or feel that it is inappropriate to become wealthy or highly compensated for what they do. I find this often with those who are dedicated to helping others—teachers of all kinds, counselors, academics, scientists, business executives, and so on. There is a big difference in power between giving and exploiting. And there is a big difference in power in being of highest and best service and taking advantage of others. You can create an intention of providing great service for which you are richly rewarded. You can describe the great service and the impact it has on the recipient, and you can describe what good you do with the rewards.

6. Allow yourself to imagine your intended reality with as many of your senses and emotions as possible.

The more senses you can bring into play, the more effective your intention is. As we learned in Chapter 5, feelings and emotions are simply thoughts manifested in the physical body. By including in your intention the feelings and emotions you are experiencing in your intended reality, you are essentially bringing that intention into physical reality.

Through self-awareness, you also can see that when you bring your senses and emotions into play, you begin to feel free. You begin to feel inspired.

Rudolf Steiner, scientific, literary, and philosophical scholar and founder of the General Anthroposophical Society, said, "Man feels truly free only in the realm of his feelings. We feel most at home when we are compelled neither by thinking nor feeling but can surrender to what is purely felt. In the sphere of feeling, we can freely experience what speaks to our soul. Feelings lie beyond our consciousness."

> *When you bring your senses and emotions into play, you begin to feel inspired.*

When others observe you stating your intentions with feeling, they notice a transformation. The tension in your face melts, your shoulders relax, your spine straightens, your chin lifts, and your eyes brighten. You look happy, at peace, and inspired. It's as though we're now observing the real you. The onion has been peeled.

As you state your intentions, choose words that are inspiring. Instead of *relationship,* use a descriptive word such as *romance* or *intimacy.* Instead of *healthy,* use words like *vibrant, vitality* and *glowing.* Instead of *great service,* use *give them the experience of a valued customer.*

The intention we wrote earlier can be rewritten to include feelings and emotions: *I am great at work, and I feel terrific. I know my strengths and the skills I bring, and I am open to learning every day. I love learning. I treat others with respect and enjoy learning from them, which adds to my effectiveness. I am open and receptive to their perspectives. Together we develop solutions. I clearly see the impact I have on the success of the organization and my colleagues. I feel confident about my performance, and my confidence builds every day. I like knowing that I am making a contribution to the organization. I feel free to be the best I can be. I smile often and laugh easily. It's contagious, and I help others enjoy their day. I enjoy helping others do a great job and be the best they can be. I notice and appreciate the contributions of others to my success, and I am thankful. I compliment them and thank them. I feel good about myself when I help others feel good about themselves.*

If you are not yet able to truly imagine your intention as reality, alternatively, you could write: *I am committed to greatness at work, and I feel terrific. I know my strengths and the skills I bring, and I am open to learning every day. I love learning. I choose respect. I choose learning. I choose openness and receptivity. I choose solutions. I choose seeing the impact I have on the success of the organization and my colleagues. I feel confident about my performance, and my confidence builds every day. I choose greatness. I choose fun. I choose helping others do a great job and be the best they can be. I notice and appreciate the contributions of others to my success. I choose thankfulness. I compliment them and thank them. I choose feeling good about myself and helping others feel good about themselves.*

If you have never thought about or written your intentions before, these examples could be a bit daunting. Some of us are more prolific than others; some of us are more flamboyant than others. Perhaps these examples seem too "touchy-feely" to you, in which case you may want to try adding details with specifics as to what you are doing and saying to fulfill the intention.

Write an intention that is comfortable and true to you. As you gain experience, you can add to it. With practice, you will find that stating your intentions becomes natural for you. For now, your intention can be just one or two sentences written in the present tense as if they are happening, in their highest way, including the impact on others as well as yourself, and with emotion and feeling.

7. Write your intention down.

Writing your intention begins the process of progressing an idea from desire to intention and the transformation of the intention from the ethereal to the physical.

You may have heard the saying that an unwritten goal is not a goal. I have found that until an intention is written, the idea is just a desire, a fancy, an intangible. Some say to me, *I don't need to write my intention. I'm very focused and clear about what I want and what I have to do, and it's all inside my head.* I used to say that too, and then I realized, much to my surprise, that until I wrote, or even stated aloud, my intention, I did not *have* an intention. Instead, I had a bunch of desires in my head. When I asked these individuals to articulate their intention, like me, they were not able to do so. They discovered that although they thought they were very focused and clear about their intentions, they were really unclear. Also, in many cases, they discovered that they did not believe their intentions could happen, or that they did not deserve the fulfillment of the intentions. Or they discovered that this wasn't really their intention at all—it was an intention they believed they *should* have.

You've no doubt experienced the power of the written intention when you were overwhelmed with all kinds of things floating around in your head that you felt you had to do. Chances are, you were so overwhelmed, you weren't getting anything done, or anything done that mattered. When you took the time to write out the to-do list, you probably felt relief as you transferred what was in your head to paper. When you finished writing the list, you probably felt confident because you experienced a knowing that these things would get done.

> *Writing your intention is one of the most powerful actions you can take.*

Writing your intention is one of the most powerful actions you can take to bring an idea or desire into reality. Over ten years ago I had a defining moment—an *aha!*

At the time, I was serving as CFO for five different companies. These were start-up companies and small, publicly traded companies in bankruptcy after having suffered from events similar to those experienced by Enron. These companies were located in several states and in Europe. And as if managing the finances of five companies wasn't enough, I bought a florist shop, a garden center, and ten greenhouses. Over a three-year period, I added two locations and grew the business 300 percent, resulting in my appearance on the cover of *Floral Management* magazine. I was working over a hundred hours per week and racking up several hundred thousand frequent flyer miles each year. I had no personal life, canceled every vacation I had planned, and rarely remembered what day of the week it was, much less whether it was a weekend.

One day, I was at my desk and my eyesight went blurry. Soon I couldn't see at all. As it turned out, I almost lost my eyesight from dehydration and suffered from a severe kidney infection. I asked myself, *What am I doing?* I began to secretly fantasize about how nice it would be to have the jobs of the people who worked with me. I even imagined working in the local bagel shop. Sure, I would make less money, I reasoned, but I could go home at night without a care in the world.

Certainly, I thought, I wouldn't go blind from working so hard.

When I reflected further, I realized that I *had* had those jobs— in high school, in college, and earlier in my career. I remembered that even then I also worked a lot of hours, canceled vacations, and managed to turn every job I had into a bigger challenge. I certainly did not go home at night without a care in the world. I then decided to look at what all those jobs had in common. And what do you think that was?

ME! I was the only common element.

I couldn't blame the job or the people I worked with or the circumstances. I was the only common thread. That was my *aha!* I realized that I was responsible for my world. Whatever position or situation I happened to be in, I created my own world.

I decided that I wanted to change my world. I realized that the only way I could change my world was to change myself. The only way to change myself was to

> *Thoughts are the only things for which we have complete responsibility and accountability.*

manage what was going on inside my head. I knew that my thoughts were the only things for which I had complete responsibility and accountability. I made a commitment to self-cultivation—the continuous improvement of myself. It was then I began my journey.

Upon reflection, I could see that throughout my life, I had chosen to manage my thoughts with excellent results in certain situations. In my adult life, I managed my thoughts with respect to major initiatives at work. I had accomplished what the accountants, lawyers, and experts said couldn't be done with the SEC, the NASD, the creditors, the customers, and the employees. I was focused on what I believed served my purpose and worked for eight hours straight without eating, going to the bathroom, or drinking water. The problem was that I was focused only on what mattered to me at work. I completely ignored the rest of my life, at work and at home.

I wondered how I could apply these practices to every area of my life. The idea came to me to write my intentions. I spent the entire weekend wondering and deciding what really mattered to me and formulating and writing my intentions. I took out a notebook and wrote down what my ideal life could be: what work I could do and what it could bring me, what kinds of clients I could have and what could they bring me, what kinds of employees and advisors I could attract, what relationships I could have at work and with my family, and what kind of person I wanted to be.

When I was finished, I looked at the intentions, and they were laughable to me. What I had written was so drastically different from the life I was living. And I believed there was no way out. It seemed ridiculous to think that these intentions were possible. So I put the notebook in a drawer.

Five years later, I found what I had written. I read the intentions, and I couldn't believe it. I was living that life. I was living my ideal life. I was dumbstruck, truly overcome. Even now, tears come to my eyes as I think about it. My ideal life was so far from the life I had been living—from which I thought there was no way out. Yet five years later, I was living that life. I experienced an *aha!* of the incredible power of the written intention.

Then came another *aha!* What if I had looked at my intentions once a year? Once a month? Once a week? Daily? *Wow!* All this time, I could have been aware of and celebrating the life I was living. What could the quality of each day be like if I was aware?

I observed that at work, I wrote down my intentions. I reviewed them frequently and accomplished what the experts said couldn't be done. *What if I applied the same practice to all aspects of my life—at work and at home?*

If you want significant results, write your intentions down and review them often. When we are mindful of our intentions, we achieve significant results.

8. Read your intention out loud, notice how you feel, and make adjustments to your intention.

Once you have written your intention, the next step is to read it out loud. If you are tempted to skip over this part, remember that it is your brain, not you, that wants to skip this. Your brain is now thinking that you're going to new heights and it might be out of a job. We all know what we do when we think we might be losing our job. We fight. We do what we can to be noticed. We point out the deficiencies of others so that we'll feel better.

You might find yourself thinking that this is corny, or stupid even, and you want to skip over it. Don't! This is a critical part of your transformation. Go somewhere private, give it a try, and discover this for yourself. You'll see how saying your intention out loud helps you home in on what is of value to you: not to others—to you. You'll feel what inspires you and what feels burdensome. You'll feel what really matters to you and not what you believe should matter. You will draw out the fears and limiting beliefs that are preventing you from putting your intention into action.

Assure your brain that it's not out of a job. Let it know that it serves a valuable function for you. It brings you information for which you can say, *Thanks, brain—I'll take it from here.*

Vocalizing your intention is another way to bring your intention from the ethereal to the physical, from thought to reality.

> *Vocalizing intentions is another way to bring our intentions from thought to reality.*

Straighten your spine, take a deep breath, exhaling deeply, and state your intention aloud three times, louder and more powerfully each time. Smile as you state your intention the second and third times. Notice any thoughts you may have as you state your intention. These thoughts are valuable insights into your subconscious thoughts. They may be signaling a limiting belief, telling you that your intention is not possible or that you may not deserve the fulfillment of your intention. Notice these thoughts without judgment or fear. Write them down and then write intentions for them, following the process we are learning in this chapter. As you write and state these additional intentions, you may discover additional thoughts that are limiting beliefs. Write down those thoughts as well and repeat the process as you peel your onion.

Notice how you feel as you state your intention. If you have a deep-seated belief that this intention is not possible or that you are not deserving of this intention, you may begin to cry. If you find yourself crying, let yourself cry. This is a good thing. A tremendous healing is in process. You are letting go of old thought patterns. Let them go. You may not even know the reason you are crying. Or you may see or feel glimpses of a past experience that is the root of your limiting belief. No matter—just keep stating your intention while breathing deeply until you are doing so without crying (and you will—it takes only a few minutes). Now state your intention while keeping your spine straight, breathing deeply, and smiling. Do this three times, louder and more powerfully each time.

Then state your intention as if you're having a conversation with someone over coffee or a beer and you're telling that person how it's going. Can you feel yourself lighten up? Can you feel yourself smiling? Can you feel your eyes lighting up? (Yes, you can feel your eyes light up.)

At this point, you may feel that your intention is so far from the reality you are currently living that you must be lying. Please be clear that you are not lying. You are speaking your truth. This is what is of significance to you. By stating your intention or writing it or thinking it, you are putting in motion the first of your *now* moments. Each time you state or write the intention, you put a new slide in your View-Master from which your brain can now begin to perceive. Your brain can now assist you, and with this new focus, it can now act and react to help you create your intended future and see that your intended future may already exist. Studies have shown that the brain doesn't know the difference between what is real, what is a memory, what is a dream, and what is being imagined. It reacts the same way and produces the same results. Without your stated intention in your View-Master, your brain continues to perceive from all of its past observations and meanings. Its projections into the future are based on the past. When you put the new slide in your View-Master by restating your intention, your brain reacts, causing behavior and producing chemicals, as if your intention is true. So while your intention is not true in the moment, stating your intention makes it true in the moment *to your brain* and it becomes reality in time. As your brain reacts, new neural nets are formed and you experience more and more moments of living your intention.

By stating and restating our intention, we create each *now* moment, and in doing so, we create our future. Eventually, you will discover that in stating an intention that may not be true right now, you are not lying at all. Instead, you are rediscovering your true nature. You may find

> *By stating and restating our intention, we create our now and our future.*

that what you thought was the truth (your current life), was in fact not true to you.

Read your intention aloud at least three times and then state it again, conversationally. Again, notice how you feel as you state your intention. This is significant—it is a big part of self-awareness. If you feel like a victim, if you feel blaming or weak, play with your intention. Rework it until you feel good, until you feel an inner power welling within you as if you're wearing a superhero cape. When your intention is powerful for you, you feel like you are *you* again. You begin to feel that it is possible to achieve this intention. Then you feel a click—a shift in yourself—a knowing that the intention is in motion. The click could come immediately, in a few hours, or after several days of stating your intention.

If you do not feel good as you state your intention, rewrite it until it feels comfortable to you. Or relax and let it come to you. Do not use force. Just as you cannot remember something when you are trying to remember and then remember it later when you have let go of the need to remember, you cannot access your higher awareness through force. Relax and let yourself open to your higher awareness. It could take two hours, two days, two weeks, or more. When it does come to you, rewrite your vision.

> *We cannot access our higher awareness through force.*

9. Think, state, and write your intention as often as possible.

Writing your vision is the most effective means to bring your intention into being. Stating it aloud is extremely powerful and the next most effective. Thinking your vision is always effective.

It is optimal to think, write, or state your intention the first thing in the morning upon waking and again at night before you sleep. These are times when you are in an in-between state of consciousness and you and your brain are most in tune with your higher awareness. You are most open and receptive to change, because you can influence the conscious and unconscious levels of your mind at the same time. By repeating your intention when you are open and receptive, you change your habits.

Most of what we think, say, and do each day is habit and is performed *unconsciously*. By being mindful of our thoughts and actions as we go through our day and by repeating our intentions when we are in a state of mindfulness, we transform our habitual thinking and behavior. By repeating our intentions, we keep them in focus. And we know that our focus creates our perceptions and our reality.

By repeating our intentions and taking the time to be quiet each day, we remain connected with our higher awareness.

You'll find that when you state your intention just before sleeping, you wake up with ideas on how to put your intention into action. You may find yourself inspired to take the next step. It's pretty amazing. Try it and see for yourself.

By repeating our intentions when we are open and receptive, we change our habits.

If I state my intentions once a year, that's great. Once a month is better. Once a week is even better. Once a day is even better. Twice a day is better still, and so on. State your intentions as often as possible.

WHAT I DO

- Once each year, I write my intentions for each area of my life.
- Almost every week or at least once a month, I reread my intentions.
- When I first awake, I think or state my intentions or only the one(s) I want to pay attention to that day.
- During the day, when I am about to enter into a situation or find myself in the middle of a situation that could benefit from the intention, or when I simply become conscious of my thoughts wandering, I either think or state aloud my intentions, depending on whether I am alone.

(continued)

> ■ When I become out of balance—anxious, nervous, fearful, angry, worried, and so on—I find it extremely empowering to repeat my intentions in thought or aloud. I regain my calm and my sense of higher purpose and service.

Any time you are mindful of your intention is a win—a huge win. It is a cause for celebration. You are now experiencing a new reality—the reality of your intention.

Thoughts of doubt, fear, and undeserving are just thoughts. They are not reality.

The following exercise provides the opportunity to practice choosing and writing your intention. Again, you may be tempted to skip this. If it is your intention to change the way you think, give it a shot. At first, I was uncomfortable and didn't want to be like the Stuart Smalley character on *Saturday Night Live* who desperately and hopelessly recited affirmations in the mirror. The real truth for me was that I didn't want to hold myself accountable. I was afraid of the thoughts I felt I knew would come, telling me I didn't deserve or couldn't fulfill the intention. You've heard the saying *The truth will set you free.* Face the truth. Face the fear. Those doubt thoughts, undeserving thoughts, and fear-of-being-held-accountable thoughts are just thoughts. They are not reality.

I invite you to practice writing your intention.

PrioriTree 4

Practice: Shaping Thought Creating and Writing My Intentions

1. **Take a deep breath and exhale deeply to access your higher awareness.**

2. **Choose what it is that you want to bring to a powerful reality and write it down.** (You can choose one of the words you identified in Chapter 7 that represents what is significant and of value to you or choose one of the unconstructive thoughts or limiting beliefs from Chapters 8 through 10 that you want to reshape,)_____.

3. **Imagine that what is significant and of value to you is now reality. Or imagine that you have let go of the unconstructlve thought or limiting belief and you have**

(continued)

new thoughts. Imagine what these new thoughts might be. Imagine that you are experiencing the reality of these new thoughts.

4. **Describe your intention—your new reality—as if it is already happening in its highest way, as if you are experiencing that reality right now. Describe what your life is like in this new reality. Write it down.** (What is your life like? What are you like? What are you doing? How are you being in the various moments of your day? What powerful impact do you make on yourself and others when you are living this vision? How do you feel—Physically? Emotionally? Spiritually?) _____.

5. **Review what you've written and make adjustments.** Have you written what you want (not what you don't want)? Have you written the intention as if it is already happening? Have you stated your intention in its highest way? Have you stated the good that results? Have you included your senses and emotions?

6. **Say it out loud and notice how you feel.** To test the power of your intention and determine if it is true to you, say it out loud. Straighten your spine, take a deep breath, exhale deeply, and state your intention aloud three times, louder and more powerfully each time. Then state your intention as if you're having a conversation with someone and you're telling that person how it's going. What do you notice? Does this feel inspiring? Does it feel good? Powerful? Can you feel yourself lighten up? Can you feel yourself smiling? Can you feel your eyes light up?

7. **Quiet yourself and notice the thoughts that come to you.** You may have thoughts of how to change the wording of your intention. In this case, go back and adjust what you have written, say it out loud again, notice, reflect, and make adjustments again until your intention feels powerful and possible. If you have thoughts of doubt, judgment, or nondeserving, create an intention for what you prefer to think. Say it out loud, notice how you feel, and make adjustments. Continue to peel your onion until you can describe how you are living that is true to you and you feel powerful, at peace, and inspired.

*It's not the answers
that show us the way,
but the questions.*

—Tennessee H. Harris

13

ASKING POWERFUL QUESTIONS

The questions we ask ourselves have a powerful impact on what we feel and what we experience every day. They powerfully affect our ability to achieve our intentions. They influence our attitudes and quality of life in general.

Take, for example, the following questions: *What's going to go wrong today? How is Dave going to stick it to me today? How will Julie screw up today?* Our *faithful-dog brain* and our reticular activation system will focus on making us right. The brain watches for and sees all the things that have gone wrong—all the examples of Dave sticking it to me or Julie screwing up. We don't see what went right—how Dave helped us today or had good intentions. We miss how we contributed to Dave's behavior or all the things that Julie did well or tried hard to do well. It becomes a self-fulfilling prophecy.

The questions we ask ourselves are key to whether we take action.

The questions we ask ourselves, and how we ask those questions, are key to whether or not we take action to fulfill an intention or how much time, energy, and money we may waste attempting to fulfill an intention. I wrote earlier about how difficult it is for many of us to decide what we want and to state our intentions in an ideal state—we think that it's impossible or that we are undeserving or selfish. Most of the people I work with, executives included, have great difficulty formulating questions in a productive way—a way that leads them toward fulfilling their intention in the most effective way and in a manner that contributes to their greatness and happiness in each moment.

I had a client whose business was growing to a new level—tripling in size in a thirty-six-month period. With this change, the organization was no longer a company of ten people who were all in the same room, able to know everything that was happening as it was happening. As a result, part of their new system involved meetings with representatives of all the functional areas to discuss and decide major issues. I attended their first meeting, and it was one of the best first meetings I had ever attended. From my perspective, it was excellent. Major issues were raised, good discussion followed, and a number of solid decisions were made. I was excited for them. I was surprised to learn that they did not share my excitement. When I spoke to a number of participants who were in the meeting, they said it was the worst meeting they had ever attended. They expressed frustration with their inability to work as a team and the inability of their president to be a leader and make tough decisions. They felt that no decisions were made at the meeting and that nothing was getting done. From my perspective, this was far from the truth. Yet here they were, demotivated, disempowered, and frustrated.

It was apparent to me that there was a big problem, and it was inside their heads. I could see that the questions they were asking were, *Will we be able to be a team? Will the president be a good leader and be able to make the tough decisions? Will we be able to change and change quickly enough? Will we survive?*

Because of the way they formulated their questions and because of the reticular activation system, their brains focused on and watched for (and I mean watched very closely for) every example where someone did not act like a team player, where the president did something that displayed less than leadership material, where something had not changed or wasn't changing fast enough, and every possible sign that they might not survive as a company.

They could not see that the good examples far outweighed the bad examples (if any bad example existed at all). They filtered out the good things, and their brains said, *See, you were right.* Then they acted accordingly, based on this information. They criticized, blamed, and acted like victims. They wasted time, energy, and money because they were not focused on their intention of being of service to their customers and to each other. And they missed out on the celebration and joy of each step they were taking as part of their exciting growth. With all of them thinking and acting this way, it was devastating for this company. It was like a cancer. It was dysfunctional. It was counterproductive to the achievement of their intention and to their well-being, both individually and as a group.

Changing the questions in our heads changes what our brains see, which changes our perceptions, which changes our experiences, which changes our focus to our intentions and what matters to us. This is how we achieve significant results.

In this instance, instead of asking, *Will we be able to be a team?* they can ask themselves, *What can I do that contributes to the success of the team?* Instead of *Will the president be able to be a leader?* they can ask, *What can I do that helps the president be a great leader?* Instead of *Will we be able to change and change*

Ask questions in a proactive way rather than a reactive way.

quickly enough? they can ask, *What can I do that accelerates change?* Instead of *Will we survive?* they can ask, *How can I help the company thrive?*

Notice that they can ask questions of themselves in a proactive rather than reactive way, which makes them personally accountable for what they can do. These questions help them to take back control instead of blaming others or being a victim. Notice that in seeking answers to these questions, they focus on the end goal. They focus on what they want—a great leader, a great team, quick change, and success—not what they don't want. They focus on what matters to them. In other words, they focus on their intentions—their purpose. They focus on managing their own thoughts, not the thoughts of others. Consequently, they control the direction of their minds to formulate answers that move them toward the achievement of their intention. Notice also that these questions bring back the state of wonder and help generate numerous ideas and possibilities of what to do and how to be.

Often, we have formed conclusions about how a parent, child, partner, colleague, boss, direct report, or customer *is,* wishing somehow that he or she didn't conform to our conclusions. We wish they were some other way—like us, for example. We ask questions like *Why are they this way? Why can't I get through to them? When will they ever ___?* or *Why don't they ___?*

For a number of reasons, asking ourselves questions in this way is not powerful. First, it does not advance anyone toward a significant result. If you have ever actually asked these questions of those about whom you've formed your conclusions, you know that not only do you not move toward the intended result, you may actually move in the opposite direction. Second, you are focused on what you don't want, because your true intent is that they *not* be a certain way. As we discussed earlier, focusing on what we do *not* want causes us to experience what we do not want. Third, when we ask *why* and *when* questions, we give away our power. We blame others. We judge them. In many cases we give away our personal accountability for the situation. We become, or at least feel, like victims, and we become powerless and may feel out of control. Fourth, when we feel like victims—powerless and out of control— we are not in a powerful state. We are not happy. We are not at peace. We are not in a state of thankfulness. We are not learning, or learning effectively. We are not creative, and we are not inspired. We may even be in fight, flight, or freeze mode.

One of my top ten favorite business books is *Corporate Lifecycles: How and Why Corporations Grow and Die and What to Do about It* by Ichak Adizes, Ph.D. In the book, Adizes points out that it is imperative to create a *"Yes we can"* climate if an organization is to thrive. In this climate, an organization can identify, analyze, and solve problems without focusing on *who* did it wrong, *when* it was done wrong, and *why* someone else did it wrong.

Our questions become powerful when we ask them in a way that regains our power and personal accountability and moves us toward the fulfillment of our intention. For example, we can ask questions like the following:

> **Powerful questions create personal accountability.**

- How can I appreciate what is special about this person and the gifts he brings?
- What questions can I ask that help me understand her perspective?
- What can I say and do right now that shows my appreciation?
- How can I learn about his needs?
- How can I be of service to her?
- What can I do that helps him meet the deadline?
- How can I be a great example?
- What can I learn from this person or this situation?

- How can I communicate my expectations?
- What can I do that makes this situation fun?
- How can I make this situation great?

Notice that these questions do not involve making other people or situations change. Instead, they all involve helping to change the world by changing ourselves. They all are asking, *What can I do?* and *How can I help?* They all involve being proactive versus reactive. They all bring about an inner peace. They all ignite creativity and move us toward significant results.

President John F. Kennedy urged his fellow citizens, "Ask not what your country can do for you; ask what you can do for your country." It's the same principle. Kennedy asked people to change their focus, take back their power, and create change.

To ask questions in a way that keeps us on purpose is powerful in and of itself. There is an even greater power achieved by asking questions in this way, and that power comes from being mindful of our purpose, our intention, and our vision. In the Introduction, I discussed how the creative portions of our brains light up when we think

> *To ask questions in a way that keeps us on purpose is powerful.*

about vision, purpose, wonder, and possibility and how the creative portions of our brains go dark when we think about blame and judgment. Have you ever been in a meeting when an idea is shot down? Did you notice the energy in the room shift downward? Have you noticed the creative energy in the room come alive when the possibilities of an idea are being bantered about? In the Introduction, I discussed how we learn most effectively when we are in a state of joy, wonder, and thankfulness. Most of us have trained ourselves to ask questions in a way that makes us feel bad. We ask questions in hindsight that bring answers highlighting what we didn't do or what went wrong. They bring about blame, judgment, and defensiveness. They do not inspire us or move us toward the fulfillment of our intention. When we ask questions in a way that reemphasizes our purpose, intention, and vision, which opens us to the sea of possibilities of fulfilling our intentions, the creative portions of our brains light up. We are open and receptive to learning. Our creative juices begin to flow, and we feel great. When we don't ask questions in this way, we feel bad. We feel like victims; we feel blaming or judgmental of ourselves and others. We feel hopeless—we are not at peace or inspired. By retraining ourselves to ask our questions in a way that makes us

> *By asking questions that inspire us and focus on what is of value, we achieve significant results and happiness.*

feel inspired and by focusing on what is of value to us, we can achieve significant results and happiness—a winning combination.

As we shape our thoughts, we can prepare questions to ask ourselves the first thing in the morning, before a meeting or a conversation, before we do a walk-through of the company, before we open the door when we go home at night, before we react to what someone is saying to us, or at the start of anything new.

SHAPING THOUGHT: ASKING POWERFUL QUESTIONS

Seven Rules of Thumb

1. Review your intention.
2. Ask questions that only you can answer.
3. Turn your questions around.
4. Ask questions in the highest way.
5. Ask how you can be of service.
6. State your questions out loud.
7. Ask your questions often.

1. Review your intention.

Reread your intention, aloud if possible. To accomplish significant results and transformation, it is helpful to formulate powerful questions that, when answered, lead you to take action toward the fulfillment of your intention.

2. Ask questions that only you can answer.

Ask questions that ask what *you* can do, not what someone else can do or what you can make someone else do. We all know that we can't make others do what we want and can't change other people. When we ask questions we can't answer, we set ourselves up to experience stress, anger, frustration, sadness, disappointment, shame, guilt, and even failure. Nor do we make any progress toward the fulfillment of our in-

When we ask questions we can't answer, we set ourselves up for failure.

tention. In fact, we may go farther in the opposite direction, fulfilling what we don't want.

Effective questions start with, *How can I ___?* or *What can I ___?* Let's use the intention that we built on in Chapter 12 to demonstrate the kinds of questions we can develop to obtain the answers that help keep us moving toward the achievement of our intention.

I am great at work and I feel terrific.

- What great thing can I do at work today?
- What can I do in this moment that brings greatness to my work?

I know my strengths and the skills I bring. I am open to learning every day. I love learning.

- How can I learn about my strengths and skills and best utilize them at work?

- What can I learn in this moment?
- How can I make learning fun?

I clearly see the impact I have on the success of the organization and on my colleagues.

- How can I learn about the goals and strategies of the organization and how my work contributes to its success?
- How can I learn about the needs of my colleagues so that I can be of great service to them, to me, and to the organization?
- How can I contribute in this moment?

I feel confident about my performance, and my confidence builds every day.

- How can I improve my performance in this moment?
- What success can I acknowledge (or celebrate) and build upon today?
- What can I do today to practice building my self-confidence?

I smile often and laugh easily. It's contagious, and I help others enjoy their day.

- How can I make this moment fun?
- What can I do that could brighten someone's day?
- How can I brighten my own day?
- What can I do today that I enjoy?
- How can I help others today?
- What can I do in this moment that helps others?

I enjoy helping others do a great job and be the best they can be. I notice and appreciate the contributions of others to my success, and I am thankful. I compliment them and thank them. I feel good about myself when I help others feel good about themselves.

- What can I do in this moment that shows others how much I appreciate their help?
- How can I convey to others that I value and respect them for what they do?
- How can I give others the experience of being listened to?

Often, we may find ourselves worried or anxious about a future possibility of something going wrong or about making a wrong decision. I find that we usually experience fear when we do not feel prepared. In these instances, there are two questions that we can ask ourselves:

- What can I do that prevents ___ from happening?
- How can I fix it if it does go wrong?

By answering these two questions, we are prepared. Also, we may discover that fixing it—if it does go wrong—is not such a big deal and that it is okay if it does go wrong.

If we are sad or disappointed about a past event, we can ask ourselves the following:

- What can I do that prevents this from happening again?
- How can I react differently if this happens again?
- What can I learn from this?
- How can I be inspired by this?

3. Turn your questions around.

Sometimes, when people are formulating their questions in a way that only they can answer, they devise questions that are really asking the rest of the world to change, which may or may not happen no matter what we do. For example, questions such as *How can I help my teenager see things my way?* and *What can I do to make our customers pay a higher price for the work we do?* are not powerful. They are thoughts of force. You are trying to change (even deny) the reality of what is. The very nature of the question produces answers that place us into fight, flight, or freeze mode because our brains interpret any answer that goes against the reality that we want to be a danger to that reality. And the reality we want may not be possible.

In our earlier example, the reality that the young man experienced was that he felt that others did not respect him. He did not feel appreciated for his contributions. When he turned this around, he could see whether a truer reality was that he did not respect or appreciate himself or that he did not respect or appreciate others. He has written his intention in a powerful way to reflect the turnaround:

I treat others with respect and enjoy learning from them, which adds to my effectiveness. I am open and receptive to their perspectives. Together we develop solutions. I clearly see the impact I have on the success of the organization and my colleagues. I feel confident about my performance, and my confidence builds every day. I like knowing that I am making a contribution to the organization.

His questions therefore do not ask what he can do to make others respect and appreciate him. Instead, he can turn his questions around and ask powerful questions to obtain answers to move him toward the fulfillment of the intention, inner peace, and happiness:

- How can I show respect to others today?
- How can I respect myself in this moment?
- What kinds of questions can I ask to understand another person's perspective?
- What can I learn from this person, this situation, or this mistake?
- How can I obtain input from others that creates solutions?

- What can I do today that acknowledges and appreciates others' great work?
- How can I acknowledge and appreciate my work?
- How can I be the best I can be?

4. Ask questions in the highest way.

We all deal with difficult people and situations every day. Did you ever notice how the more we want a situation or a person to go away, it, he, or she just keeps coming back? It's like the movie *Groundhog Day*!

How many times have we said things like *I would be happy except that the owner, my child, a coworker, or my partner is such a jerk* or *If only ___ would stop ___, I would be happy*?

If we are focused on true success in the long haul, we do not let these thoughts rule our world. We do not waste our valuable time and energy being negatively affected by people and situations. Instead, we remain focused on what matters to us and on our intention. We are focused on our own self-cultivation, which is the continuous improvement of ourselves.

As we encounter difficult people and situations, we know that what we have is another lesson, another challenge, another learning experience, another chance to serve as an example, to set the tone, to cement the culture and values of our company or our families. In other words, we have an opportunity to refocus on our intention and be on purpose.

> *As we encounter challenging people and situations, we can develop questions that keep us on purpose.*

If we are firm in the knowing that *I change the world around me by changing myself,* we do not depend on someone or something else to change in order for us to be happy or for our families or organizations to be successful. Instead of being reactive and dependent on someone else for our happiness or success, we are proactive and take charge by managing our thoughts. We change our focus.

As we encounter challenging people and situations, we can develop questions so that our *faithful-dog brains* bring us constructive answers:

- How can I be of service in this situation or to this person?
- What new thought can I practice?
- What can I learn from this experience or from this individual?
- How can I change my procedures or my approach to the situation or this individual?
- How can I change my perception?
- How can I learn this lesson in a joyous way?
- What can I do that makes this situation a great one?
- What can I do that makes this situation fun?
- How can I, in this moment, contribute to the greater good? (The greater good could be the relationship, the long-term vision, the culture, a person's development, the example you want to set, or another goal.)
- What can I be thankful for in this situation? Or about this person?

When we ask questions that help us see what is good about a person or a situation, the answers we seek raise us to a high level of thinking. The higher the level of our thinking, the greater our success.

When I went into turnaround situations, I used to ask what was wrong with the company, the industry, the strategy, and the people. Then I worked on implementing changes to fix them. When I changed my questions to ask them in a highest way, asking about what is right, what is possible, and what we could do to fulfill our vision, I experienced a far greater result. The turnarounds were almost immediate; everyone was engaged and inspired and generated exciting new ideas.

In hindsight, it's easy to see the reason for the dramatic difference. When I asked what was wrong, my focus—and therefore the focus of everyone in the company—was on what was wrong. The focus on what was wrong contributed to bad morale. Blame and judgment persisted, and everyone's creativity was squelched. The creative regions of their brains were darkened. We were never catching anybody doing anything right, and as a result, we were not in a state of joy and thankfulness. Again, our creativity was squelched, and our ability to learn effectively was severely hampered. It is no wonder that when we focused on what was great, what was possible, vision and purpose, we operated in a higher way, focused on what truly matters, and functioned in a state of joy and thankfulness. The creative juices could now flow.

> *Ask what is right about the situation to produce answers that build upon strengths and achieve greatness.*

By asking questions in the highest way, we produce answers that build upon strengths to achieve greatness. Things that are *wrong,* that is, inconsistent with our intention, dissipate because they are no longer part of our nature, or they became very easy to fix.

5. Ask how you can be of service.

How can I be of service? is the be-all and end-all of questions. We first learn to ask this question in a spiritual sense in Sunday school. I have found this question to bring about great success in the secular areas of work and in life.

Organizations are born to satisfy a need, and they die because they fail to satisfy needs. Organizations that are successful satisfy the needs of their stakeholders—the customers, investors, suppliers, and employees. To stay successful, they are constantly changing because the needs of their stakeholders are constantly changing. Successful organizations are constantly shaping their thoughts and asking the question *How can I be of service?*

The organizations that ultimately fail ask questions that lead to blame and judgment, such as, *What's in it for me? Why did you do this? Who made the mistake?* You'll also hear people saying things like *This is the way we've always done it. They're lucky to have a job here. If they want to do business with us, they'll have to do it our way. I'm not going to invest any time or effort in learning what the market wants, I just want to milk this.*

We can always ask how we can be of service.

Organizations are living organisms, just as we are. We too are successful when we are of service to our stakeholders. We too have customers (our chil-

> **We are successful when we are of service to our stakeholders.**

dren, our colleagues, our parents, and our partners). We have suppliers and employees (our children's teachers, anyone who assists or contributes to our education, our livelihood, our sustenance, our security, and our well-being). We have investors (our employers, our managers, our partners, our spouses, our parents, our shareholders, and our lenders).

How can you be of service to your stakeholders?

I had been working for several years with a financially troubled client when we began to work on a deal with new investors. The new investors wanted to take on management control of my client. Their financial advisor wanted to run the company and disparaged me to the new investors, who informed me that once the deal was done, I would be let go as chief financial officer and replaced by the financial advisor.

At first I was upset and judgmental. I didn't respect the bad-mouthing: *Oh, this is such inappropriate behavior!* My upset built as I held on to victim thoughts: *I have worked so hard with this company during its bad times, and now I won't be involved during the good times.* I then moved on to, *Well, if I am going to help during the transition, then they better pay me big bucks.*

At this point I had definitely lost sight of my intention. I had also given away my power. I had chosen to be a victim, to be reactive, and to experience thoughts and emotions that were not constructive for me. I was miserable, and my health began to suffer. After several weeks, I gained my composure and asked myself, *How can I be of service?* The employees of the company had worked so hard, and it would be wonderful for them to have these new investors. So I decided to continue to work on the project and do my best to feel compassion for the financial advisor who had the need to belittle my efforts. I decided to feel compassion for the new investors, who were acting on misinformation. I chose not to worry about the money and focus on being of highest and best service.

When the deal was done, the new investors gave me a handsome bonus. They increased my fee and paid me severance, which they were under no obligation to do. They engaged me to help them on other projects at an increased fee. Another officer in the company was in the same situation. He continued to be upset. He made demands for money and was not helpful. I later learned that he was terminated without severance.

I changed the world around me by changing myself. I asked constructive questions: *How can I be of service? What is my intention?* The following story shows how we can always ask, *How can I be of service?*

A Service Lesson

Sandy, an administrative assistant, was upset over the behavior of a manager at her company, Joe, who yelled and screamed at her because the copy machine was out of paper. Even though the copy machine was not Sandy's responsibility, she felt there was nothing she could do in this situation other than suffer the vehemence of Joe's tirade. Sandy wanted to remain on task at work and have others recognize that she had an important job to do and deadlines to meet. She was upset even as she recalled the story. I asked her if it was really true that she could do absolutely nothing in this situation. She said, "Yes." I said, "Really? There was nothing you could do?" Again she said, "Yes."

Often, we feel there is nothing we can do, when in reality we have a variety of options, including choosing to do nothing. As we talked about in Chapter 6, when we believe there is nothing we can do, we do not see the many possible alternative actions available to us. Sandy could at least ask herself how she could be of service to herself, to Joe, or to others in this situation. She could find a number of choices about what she could think, say, and do.

How can she be of service to herself? By choosing to remain in her power and by choosing to remain happy and at peace. She can choose to remember that Joe's behavior has nothing to do with her and not take his behavior personally. She can choose to take a deep breath and feel compassion for Joe, who is so out of balance that he is screaming at someone who isn't even responsible. She can choose to be of service to Joe by calmly saying to him, "Joe, I know how upsetting it can be when the copier runs out of paper, especially when you're in a hurry." When upset people feel that they have been listened to and that their feelings have been acknowledged or validated, they often calm down. If Sandy remains calm and peaceful and is filled with compassion, her energy is more powerful than Joe's. In this instance, Joe either rises to her level and calms down or goes to find someone else to scream at.

Sandy can also be of service to herself and to Joe by calmly saying, "Joe, I have a deadline to meet. I know that Sue is responsible for the

(continued)

copier. Let's call her now. I'm sure she'll be happy to help." Together they could make the call to Sue. Or Sandy could say, "Joe, I'm on a tight deadline too, and I'm not responsible for the copier. I think I can show you what to do." And then she could proceed to show Joe what needs to be done to correct the situation, being of service to Joe and to herself, after making a conscious choice to do so.

Sandy could also be of service to herself by letting the incident go. Sandy had chosen to assume that Joe's behavior meant that she was not respected, which is not true. Joe's behavior has nothing to do with whether her deadlines matter. It was not Joe's behavior that bothered Sandy; it was Sandy's thinking about Joe's behavior that bothered her. She could choose to let the thought go and remain focused on her priorities.

Sandy could also choose to be of service to herself by visiting Joe an hour later or the next day and mentioning in a friendly, caring way, "Joe, I want to talk to you about our interchange. I know you were very upset, and even though I am not responsible for the copier and had my own deadlines to meet, in the best interests of your client and the company and you, and because I'm a great person (she can smile and laugh here), I helped you out with the copier. I did want you to know, in case this happens again, that Sue is responsible for the copier. I put a sign up in the copy room with her name and extension." Through this conversation, Sandy is of service to herself, to Joe, and to others. She can be happy and at peace and fulfill her intention of being on task at work.

Without blame or judgment, Sandy could also say, "Joe, I know that you are a manager here and want to do a great job. I thought it might be helpful for you to know that you could get more help and support from me and others if you calmly and nicely asked for help." Or Sandy could just let it go and wish him well in her head and heart.

We always have many choices. I find that the fewer choices I think I have, the more choices I actually do have. When we are calm, peaceful, and mindful of our intention, we know the right thing to do.

6. State your questions out loud.

State your questions out loud and practice self-awareness as you ask yourself the questions. How do you feel? If asking your question makes you feel bad, like a victim, stressed, uninspired, blaming, or judging, rework your question until it feels good to you. If you notice that your eyebrows are furrowed; your neck, chest, or gut is tight; your heartbeat is fast; or your breaths are short, rework your question until it feels good to you. When your question is framed powerfully, you feel powerful. You feel focused. You feel open, receptive, and creative. You feel good.

You are best served by questions that bring you back to your state of wonder, curiosity, creativity, and imagination. Your questions need not cause a feeling of being driven or forced. Many people ask, *What do I need to do to ___?* Asking the question in this way results in a feeling of pressure, self-judgment, and being driven. The question does not bring peace. It does not inspire. It does not ignite creativity. It actually squelches creativity and inspiration. Ask instead, *What step(s) can I take today or in this moment that ___? What can I learn about ___ so I can ___?*

Restating action items in the form of a question invokes our creativity and imagination.

Along this same line, I find it helpful for companies and individuals to restate goals and action items in the form of a question or in a state of wonder. Have you noticed how you feel when you look at your list of goals, items on your action plan, or your to-do list? Do you feel inspired? Do you feel like this is going to be fun? Few people are inspired. Few people feel a sense of wonder, power, or purpose as they read their lists. Most people report that they feel bad. They feel burdened and obligated to do yet another thing. Many tend to procrastinate, or they have great trouble being creative about how to do it.

Restating your action items in the form of a question brings about significant results. Instead of *Increase market share by 10 percent* or *We need to increase market share,* ask, *How can we increase market share?* or say, *I wonder how we can increase market share.* Feel the difference. Notice what happens. Instead of stating, *Exercise five times a week,* or *I need to exercise five times a week,* ask, *What five ways can I exercise this week?* or say, *I wonder how I can exercise this week.* Feel the difference. See what happens.

7. Ask your questions often.

The more frequently you ask yourself your questions, the sooner you begin to seek the answers and initiate action. In addition, your brain becomes focused on noticing the answers to your questions. Ask your questions the first thing in the morning and before you sleep so that your conscious and un-

> *Put questions in your tool kit to have ready for the times your thinking may be challenged.*

conscious minds seek the answers. Put questions in your tool kit to have ready for the times your thinking may be challenged. Exhale deeply, then take a deep breath and ask the question immediately before a situation that pertains to your questions. For example, if my intention is vibrant health, as I am standing at the all-you-can-eat buffet, I can ask myself, *Which healthy foods can I choose to eat right now?* If my intention is a work environment that fosters great communication, before I go into a meeting, write an e-mail, or make a phone call, I can ask myself, *What questions can I ask to learn the team members' perspectives? What can I do that gives them the experience of being listened to? How can I communicate my expectations?*

When we are continually mindful of our intentions and ask questions that move us another step toward the achievement of our intentions, we achieve significant results.

The next exercise provides practice in developing powerful questions.

PrioriTree 5

Practice: Shaping Thought
Asking Powerful Questions

1. **Choose the intention you want to bring to a powerful reality and write it down.** Remember to describe your new reality as if it is already happening in its highest way—as if you are experiencing that reality right now. Describe what your life is like in this new reality: What is your life like? What are you like? What powerful impact do you make on yourself and others when you are living this vision? How do you feel—Physically? Emotionally? Spiritually?

_____

_____

_____

_____

(continued)

2. **Review what you've written and write the success factors to achieve this intention**. Think for a moment of the success factors for achieving this vision. As an example, for achieving vibrant health, you may feel that the success factors are eating natural whole foods, enjoying regular aerobic exercise, taking time to rejuvenate and relax each day, and being appreciative of yourself. For another example, let's say you have an important meeting with a potential customer. You may feel the success factors are that you have identified the pain of the potential customer, you have successfully related your capabilities and solutions with that pain, you have identified a champion, and you have determined what could cause that customer to choose you.

_____

_____

_____

_____

3. **Formulate How can I? and What can I do? questions that include your success factors**. For the vibrant health example, you might ask, What natural whole food can I eat this week? What day of the week or what meal each day can I eat that's filled with natural whole foods? What aerobic activity can I enjoy today or this week? How can I relax today? How can I relax in this moment? What about me am I thankful for? For the meeting with the potential customer, you might ask yourself, How can I create an atmosphere of trust? What questions can I ask that dig deep and find the pain? What information about us can I share that relates to that pain? How can I find out who the decision maker is? I wonder what their decision matrix entails? How can I prepare for this meeting? How can I be of highest and best service to this potential customer?

_____

_____

_____

_____

4. **State your questions out loud and notice how you feel as you ask your questions**. If you do not feel empowered, if you feel pressured, like a victim, hopeless, judgmental, or blaming, then reformulate your questions.

_____

_____

_____

_____

Be impeccable with your word.
Regardless of what language you speak,
your intent manifests through the word.

What you dream, what you feel,
and what you really are,
will all be manifested
through the word.

—Don Miguel Ruiz

14

MAKING POWERFUL
STATEMENTS

We shape our thoughts by choosing our intentions and by asking ourselves powerful questions. We also shape our thoughts with the statements we make to ourselves inside our heads.

Do you chant a mantra? Even if your answer is no, you have never meditated in your life, I say that your answer is yes. We make statements to ourselves all day long. Each time we make a statement to ourselves, we are repeating our mantra. Each time we repeat our mantra, we move it deeper and deeper into our subconscious. Each time we repeat our mantra, we program ourselves, building and strengthening our neural net. The more often we think the same thoughts in relation to each other, the more often we reinforce our neural net, and the stronger those ideas become.

As we learned in Chapter 9, viewing events and surroundings through our View-Master affects our focus, which affects our perception, which creates our reality. We can redirect the focus of our minds to move us toward the fulfillment of our intention. We can create new slides for our View-Master by choosing the thoughts that rule our world and by choosing the statements we make to ourselves.

We can choose to make powerful statements to ourselves. Powerful statements are those that remind us of our intentions and of what serves our purpose. Powerful statements reinforce our purpose and support our intentions. As we go about our day and experience what others do

> *Powerful statements reinforce our purpose and support our intentions.*

and say, we can consciously choose to make powerful statements to ourselves that remind us of how we choose to think, feel, act, or react. As situations unfold at work and in life, we do not waste time, energy, or money being upset over someone's behavior. We do not need to prove ourselves right and others wrong or make ourselves winners. We no longer make decisions or act in ways that move us away from what we truly want to accomplish. We do not waste time or energy criticizing, judging, or blaming. We can choose to make powerful statements to remain firmly grounded and centered on our intentions—on what truly matters to us.

Let's revisit the young man's intention that was developed in Chapter 12:

I am great at work, and I feel terrific. I know my strengths and the skills I bring, and I am open to learning every day. I love learning. I treat others with respect and enjoy learning from them, which adds to my effectiveness. I am open and receptive to their perspectives. Together we develop solutions. I clearly see the impact I have on the success of the organization and my colleagues. I feel confident about my performance, and my confidence builds every day. I feel free to be the best I can be. I smile often and laugh easily. It's contagious, and I help others enjoy their day. I enjoy helping others do a great job and be the best they can be. I notice and appreciate the contributions of others to my success, and I am thankful. I compliment them and thank them. I feel good about myself when I help others feel good about themselves.

Or alternatively:

I am committed to greatness at work, and I feel terrific. I know my strengths and the skills I bring, and I am open to learning every day. I love learning. I choose respect. I choose learning. I choose openness and receptivity. I choose solutions. I choose seeing the impact I have on the success of the organization and my colleagues. I feel confident about my performance, and my confidence builds every day. I choose greatness. I choose fun. I choose helping others do a great job and be the best they can be. I notice and appreciate the contributions of others to my success. I choose thankfulness. I compliment them and thank them. I choose feeling good about myself and helping others feel good about themselves.

Note that these intentions contain powerful statements to reinforce values and purpose and support the intention of being great at work and feeling fulfilled. What this young man can do is pull one or two of the sentences from his intention to serve as powerful statements. He can put these into his *Managing Thought* tool kit to use as the need arises throughout the day. So, before he goes into a meeting or makes a phone call or as he thinks thoughts that he's not great at work, he might say, *I am free to be the best I can be,* or he may choose to remind himself that no matter what he feels or thinks, he can choose to act in a peaceful and respectful way because he is in service of these values—for example, *I choose respect, I choose peace,* or *I choose learning.*

Your tool kit can include powerful questions or powerful statements.

He may choose other powerful statements. For example, let's say that this young man's job requires interaction with people in other departments whom he would rather not work with because he feels that they are condescending or pompous. His tool kit for this particular interaction can include powerful questions and powerful statements. For some of us, it feels powerful to use questions; for others, it feels powerful to use statements. In some situations, questions may feel more powerful than statements, and in other situations, statements may feel powerful. It is up to us to choose which thoughts bring us the most power. As an example, this young man's tool kit might include any number of the following thoughts:

- A reminder to himself of his intention:
  I am great at work and feel terrific or *I choose greatness.*
- A powerful question to himself:
  What can I learn from Joe today?
  How can I show my appreciation to Joe for the knowledge he has and shares with me?
- A deep breath, and a powerful statement to himself:
  I treat Joe with respect (or *I respect Joe*).
  I enjoy learning from Joe. I am open and receptive to his perspective.
  I use this interaction to learn about Joe and myself.
  I choose openness. I choose receptivity. I choose learning.

You can prepare a tool kit for each interaction or situation that presents a challenge or roadblock to fulfilling your intention. Because we tend to live each day as we did yesterday and think the same thought patterns over and over again, through self-awareness you can *watch* your thoughts and *see* the thoughts you have each day relating to particular individuals and situations. You will notice patterns. You can, through self-awareness, ask yourself and determine which thoughts are constructive to your intentions and which are not, which thoughts serve your purpose and which do not. You can choose the thoughts you want to have. You can prepare your tool kit of powerful statements and powerful questions to replace the unconstructive or destructive thoughts as, or even before, they occur. You can practice using powerful statements in your tool kit until you have transformed your thoughts, actions, and reactions.

Does this mean you can choose all your thoughts? No. Although you may significantly reduce the frequency of some of your initial thoughts, it's likely that you may still have a worry thought, fear thought, or whatever thoughts have been predominant for you. Your tool kit can be prepared and at the ready for the moment you observe the initial thought.

Your powerful statements are the tools you can use to create your reality, adjust your thinking, and rewire your neural net. As you create your statements, take several deep breaths and exhale deeply to calm and center yourself and remind yourself of your

Powerful statements move us to take action.

intention. Then develop powerful statements that support your intention and move you to take action toward the fulfillment of your intention.

Let's examine the first attempt at a powerful statement developed by a participant in a *Managing Thought* workshop: *I stay calm so I won't eat foods that are filled with fat and are bad for me.*

The first thing to notice is that this statement is not proactive and, in fact, is counterproductive, even destructive. Making this statement keeps him focused on everything he does not want. Because of the reticular activation system that we discussed in Chapter 8, he continually focuses on and notices the negative elements of the statement—fat-filled foods that are bad for him. He notices all the times he ate the bad, fat-filled foods. He is not focused on the foods that are good for him. He does not notice any of the good food choices he has made. Not only is he unable to celebrate the progress he has made, he does not develop a momentum of success. Instead, he spends his day suffering as he notices the bad foods and tries to avoid them. He does not fulfill his intention. He continues to reinforce his neural net to notice and eat bad foods and be angry with himself. It was easy to see that he felt bad as he read the statement.

The rules of thumb for creating your intention in Chapter 12 apply equally to powerful statements and are fundamental to making your powerful statements proactive.

SHAPING THOUGHT: MAKING POWERFUL STATEMENTS

Nine Rules of Thumb

1. Frame your powerful statement proactively.
2. State your powerful statement in its highest way.
3. Frame your powerful statement in the active, present tense.
4. Focus your powerful statement on *being* rather than *doing*.
5. State the good that results as you live your powerful statement.
6. Allow yourself to imagine your intended reality with as many of your senses and emotions as possible.
7. Write your powerful statement down.
8. Read your powerful statement out loud, notice how you feel, and make adjustments to your powerful statement.
9. Think, state, and write your powerful statement as often as possible.

Decide what you want and express your powerful statement in its ideal state, in its highest, greatest way, and in your own style. I asked the gentleman, if he wasn't eating bad, fatty foods, what did he want to be eating? He said he wanted to eat

healthy foods—foods that would make him feel good physically and increase his energy. He added that he wanted to be calm, because when he's agitated, he tends to eat bad foods. Here are the new, powerful statements he wrote: *I am calm. I choose foods that are healthy for me.*

I asked him how he could feel if he was choosing and eating healthy foods. He developed an additional powerful statement: *I feel terrific and enjoy the energy these healthy foods bring me.*

Then he said anxiously, "I have never been able to be calm. It's very difficult for me." I reminded him that this is a limiting belief for him, that in fact, he is able to be calm and it can be very easy to be calm. We talked about the practice of breathing deeply. He crafted an additional statement: *It's easy for me to be calm. I relax with every deep breath I take.*

Alternatively, his powerful statements could simply be *I choose peace. I choose calm. I choose healthy eating.*

As he read his statements aloud, everyone in the room could see the transformation. His eyes lit up, he smiled, his face and body relaxed, and his back straightened. He had regained his power.

In this state of power, he feels happy and at peace, and he learns most effectively. In this state, the creative portion of his brain is working. He can now focus on being calm and on making healthy food choices. He will ask powerful questions: *What can I do right now (or today) to be calm and at peace? What foods can I eat today (or right now) that are healthy for me? Which meal can I eat each day that is healthy?* He is rewiring his neural nets.

PrioriTree 6

Practice: Shaping Thought Creating Powerful Statements

Test Your Powerful Statement

Once you have written your powerful statement, test it by reading it aloud. Straighten your spine, exhale deeply, and then repeat the statement three times. Now reread the statement while breathing naturally and smiling.

Notice any thoughts that come to you as you are making the statement—thoughts that represent limiting beliefs or self-defeating statements. For each of these thoughts, think of the

Read your powerful statement out loud. Notice how you feel.

thoughts you could prefer to have and write an additional powerful statement to replace these thoughts. Again, notice how you feel. You may feel like crying. If you do, allow yourself to cry. A tremendous healing is in place. Then keep repeating the statement until you can do so without crying. Repeat your powerful statement until you can say it while smiling. If you find that you do not feel powerful as you vocalize your statement, rewrite it until it feels comfortable. If you find that you feel like a victim or sense that you are in a blaming or judgmental mode as you reread your statement, rewrite it. If you find you feel burdened or forced; your eyebrows are furrowed; your neck, chest, and gut are tight; or your breaths are short as you reread your statement, rewrite it.

The trick is to relax, invoke the state of wonder, and let it come to you, let it flow. If your intentions are sincere and you are clear on the good that results from the fulfillment of your intentions, you will find that as you repeat your statement, you begin to feel a better way to word your powerful statement. As you progress in the fulfillment of your intention, this is particularly true. This knowing could come right away, in two hours, two days, two weeks, or more. It *will* come to you, and when it does, rewrite your powerful statement.

As an example, one woman developed the statement *I am willing to change.* While she understood the meaning of *free beer tomorrow* (see Chapter 12) and the *being versus observing* rule of thumb, she did not feel comfortable at all with any statement other than *I am willing to change.*

I know that she could have rewritten the statement. And I know that although she might have cried as she vocalized the statement, she could have released her fear and regained her power. She could have felt the very real possibility of the new reality. Yet she couldn't do it. Not then.

She was sincere in her intention. She was very clear on the good that could come from fulfilling her intention, and so I advised her to continue to use her statement and see what happened. About a month later she called me to say that as she was making her statement, the thought came to her that she could make her statement in a more powerful way. She felt very good about it and very safe.

Be sincere in your intention. Be clear on the good that arises by fulfilling your intention. Say

> *Be sincere in your intention.*

your powerful statement out loud. Breathe. Smile. See how you feel. See what comes to you. Rewrite your powerful statements. Write new powerful statements as you peel your onion.

The following are examples of some powerful statements I have used.

POWERFUL STATEMENTS

I am happy.

I am open and receptive. I seek to understand.

I do my best in everything I do.

I am thankful for all my blessings, all that I am, and all that I have.

I am thankful for the contribution of countless others to my livelihood, my education, my dwelling, my sustenance, my well-being, and my success.

I serve others to the best of my ability in all I say and do.

I make the most of my time each and every day.

(continued)

I am a wonderful success in all of my undertakings.

My work is a great contribution to others, and I am richly rewarded.

I accept prosperity in my life and allow myself to have more than I can ever dream possible.

My prosperity prospers others; I send others thoughts of their increased prosperity.

Money flows freely in my life. I always have more money coming in than going out.

My money is a source of good for me and for others.

I attract to me only those things that bless and prosper me.

Energy flows freely in every area of my life. All my energy exchanges are positive.

I create things easily and effortlessly.

I change the world around me by changing myself.

I hold only constructive, powerful, and loving thoughts.

I am true to my word.

I feel strong and powerful as I take consistent action to accomplish my purpose.

I am willing to change and to grow. I am safe to create a new future.

Today is a new and wonderful day. I make the most of every moment.

I release all blame and accept the peace and joy of life.

I feel the joy of life as I use my power to benefit myself and others.

I love and trust the flow and the process of life. I am safe.

I lovingly release the past and turn my attention to this new day.

I love and approve of myself. I am at peace. I am calm. All is well.

I am filled with love, compassion, and forgiveness.

I forgive others. I forgive myself.

I love and enjoy life.

I love myself, my humanity, my divinity, and all my thoughts, feelings, emotions, and fears.

I bring love and a positive attitude to everything I do.

I demonstrate love in every action every day.

I acknowledge how far I've come.

I affirm my commitment to my higher purpose and my world service.

My higher purpose and world service are my highest priority.

I live a life of joy and aliveness, filled with loving relationships, peace, prosperity, abundance, and love.

I am in perfect health, and the law of harmony operates in my mind, body, and soul.

I pray for lives of joy and aliveness, filled with loving relationships, peace, prosperity, abundance, love, and perfect health for my family, friends, colleagues, and all people everywhere.

I choose peace.

I choose prosperity.

I choose gratitude.

I choose service.

I choose balance.

I choose joy.

I choose kindness.

I choose openness and receptivity.

I choose creativity.

I choose expansiveness.

I choose love.

I choose forgiveness.

I choose compassion.

I choose greatness.

I choose leadership.

I choose truth.

I choose abundance.

I choose balance.

I choose power.

I now . . .

I now practice . . .

I wonder what I can . . .

I wonder . . .

Practice Makes Permanent

It is optimal to think, write, or state your powerful statement upon waking or before you fall asleep, when you and your brain are most open and receptive. As I mentioned earlier, most of what we think, say, and do each day is a habit and is performed *unconsciously* and consciously. By repeating our powerful statements

Practicing our powerful statements upon waking and before falling asleep moves us toward the reality we want.

when we are open and receptive, we can bring what has become *unconscious* to awareness. By repeating our powerful statements throughout the day when we are in a state of mindfulness, we can rewire our habitual thinking and behavior. By repeating our powerful statements, we keep our powerful statements in focus. We then change what we say, feel, and experience. We make good choices and act and react in a way that moves us toward the reality we want.

During the day, I repeat my powerful statements when I am about to enter into a situation that could benefit from my choosing to *be* that way. When I am caught off-guard by a person or a situation, I stop and take a drink of water (I always have water with me), and while drinking, I repeat to myself my powerful statement. If the day is really tough, I shut my door (if I have one), or go into the ladies room and repeat my powerful statements. I regain my calm and my sense of higher purpose and service. I regain my power and focus.

An affirmation will not work if it is not sincere, is not believed, cannot be imagined, or serves as a distraction.

At this point, some people tell me that powerful statements are affirmations and affirmations do not work. Some say that from their own experience they *know* that affirmations do not work. Others cite clinical proof that they do not work.

I offer this as food for thought. Powerful statements, affirmations, invocations, prayer—whatever you choose to call them—do not work if the statements are not sincere. A statement is not sincere when it is not believed, when it cannot be imagined, or when its true purpose is to serve as a distraction or a denial of what is. As an example, let's assume that we become upset by someone's behavior that is abusive toward us. If we affirm, *I am at peace* or *I attract loving relationships,* these affirmations will not work if we cannot imagine or believe in the possibility of peace or loving relationships. If we say *I am at peace* repeatedly, with the intention to mask or distract us from our true feelings, again, the intention or affirmation is not sincere and will not work. If we say *I am at peace* or *I attract loving relationships* and we are denying what is—for example, we're in an abusive relationship—instead of acknowledging what is, being thankful for the lessons learned from the experience, and then affirming commitment to a new direction, the affirmation or intention will not work. If we cannot see what is, for example, intending to go east looking for a sunset, the affirmation will not work. It is comforting to note that when we are calm and sincere, we will *know* in which direction to look for the sunset.

If we cannot imagine or believe the affirmation or intention, the next best steps are to affirm our choice or commitment to move in the direction that serves our purpose, for example, *I choose peace* or *I choose loving relationships.* Or we can ask powerful questions that guide us to the direction of our intentions, such as *How can I find peace in this moment?* or *How can I attract a loving relationship?* Or we can invoke the state of wonder to help us determine or imagine our vision of peace or loving relationships.

Remember, just a few powerful, constructive thoughts a day far outweigh all of the weak, nonconstructive, and fearful thoughts you may have. If you state your intentions and powerful statements once a year, that's great. The more you state your intentions and statements, the sooner your new way of thinking becomes natural for you. It is the practice and repetition that reshapes your thoughts.

Any time you repeat your powerful statements and questions, it is a win—a huge win—and a cause for celebration, because each time you repeat your powerful statements and questions, you are choosing a new reality. Your new reality is in process. You are experiencing your new reality. You are rewiring your neural nets. You are in service of your purpose. You are moving in the direction of your dreams.

> *Each time you repeat your powerful statements and questions, you are choosing a new reality.*

Our lives are like a chess game.
The move of a single pawn
affects the outcome of the game.

—David R. Hawkins, MD, Ph.D.

15

REPLACING WEAK THOUGHT PATTERNS WITH POWERFUL THOUGHT PATTERNS

W e shape our thoughts by choosing our intentions, asking ourselves powerful questions, and making powerful statements to ourselves. We also shape our thoughts by replacing weak thought patterns with powerful thought patterns.

I mentioned earlier in reference to the book *Power vs. Force* by David R. Hawkins, MD, Ph.D., that the energy of thought can be measured and that "the difference in power between a loving thought and a fearful thought is so enormous as to be beyond the capacity of the human imagination to easily comprehend." When I first read this, I was taken aback. I experienced an incredible *aha!* Until that moment, I approached my work and my own self-cultivation by looking for what was wrong and then working on making it right. Even under the guise of continuous improvement or self-cultivation, I looked for what could be improved (what was wrong) and worked on making it better (right). In managing my own thought, I focused on getting rid of negative, weak, and forceful thoughts, which kept me focused on the thoughts I did not want. I became very critical of others and myself as I noticed *wrong* thoughts, and I did not notice or celebrate my *good* thoughts. I missed out on the joy of my life, my work, and my expansiveness.

When I learned that the difference in power between a *bad* thought and a *good* thought was so enormous as to be beyond my comprehension, I realized how just a few powerful, constructive, loving thoughts a day far outweigh all my weak, nonconstructive, and fearful thoughts. When I learned that the scale is logarithmic, so that a change of five points can make an enormous difference in personal power, I realized that I could be far more effective in work and in life by focusing on what is good. I realized that I could transform my thinking and my reality by focusing on the powerful thoughts I want to have and not the weak thoughts I don't want to have. I could also see how just one more powerful thought a day would have a logarithmic effect on my personal power.

Another big *aha!* for me was learning that what I considered to be less virtuous *bad* thoughts were neither good nor bad. They were merely a function of viewpoint, which is the accumulation of my thought patterns. I realized that *everyone's* thoughts and behavior are a function of their viewpoints—

> *Everyone's thoughts and behavior are a function of their viewpoint.*

a function of their perceptions. I realized that perception is reality. I realized there is no need for me to judge or compare myself to others or to my past selves, no need to take things personally, and no need to get upset over someone else's behavior. And if I do, there is no need to hang on to these thoughts and let them rule my world.

The biggest *aha!* for me was the realization that by lifting my thoughts higher and higher each day, *I make a difference.* Until then, I was frustrated because I really wanted to make a difference. I questioned whether my job, my career path, or the widgets manufactured by the company I was involved with made a difference. Then I realized that the more I increase my personal power, with just small improvements each day, the more I am able to help others and be happy, joyful, and peaceful. I can change the world around me by changing myself.

We increase our inner power as we accept responsibility for every thought, word, and deed we generate.

Read the following list of pairs of qualities. Reflecting on them can help raise our level of consciousness and improve the quality of our thought patterns, lifting our thoughts higher and higher each day. When we are aware of the distinctions between powerful and weak thought patterns, we increase our inner power as we make each choice of who and how to be and as we accept responsibility for every thought, word, and deed we generate. I find this list extremely helpful in examining my belief systems, increasing my understanding of my deep personal values and definitions of success, and reflecting on whether what I am thinking or doing is empowering.

Notice what thoughts come to you as you review the list.

POWERFUL VS. WEAK THOUGHT PATTERNS

Concerned . . . Judgmental		Observant . . . Suspicious	
Courageous . . . Reckless		Praising . . . Flattering	
Experienced . . . Cynical		Purposeful . . . Desirous	
Helpful . . . Meddling		Reliant . . . Dependent	
Leading . . . Coercing		Striving . . . Struggling	

Reprinted with permission from David R. Hawkins, MD, Ph.D., *Power vs. Force*, Veritas Publishing, www.veritaspub.com

There is a difference between being confident and being arrogant; one is powerful, and one is weak. There is a difference between being honest and legal, educating and persuading, significant and important, diplomatic and deceptive, determined and stubborn, and thankful and indebted.

I remember giving a presentation on networking. Some of the participants thought networking is brownnosing (force). Networking can be powerful when the true spirit of giving and receiving is invoked.

We can choose to replace weak thought patterns with powerful thought patterns and in so doing increase our personal power. Increasing our personal power increases our level of consciousness, which powerfully influences our lives and the lives of others. The higher our level of con-

> *Increasing our consciousness powerfully influences our lives and the lives of others.*

sciousness, the higher our vibration and the more interested we are in the well-being and spiritual awareness of others. Also, the higher and lighter the vibration, the healthier and happier we are. The lower and denser the vibration, the more unhealthy and unhappy we are. Buddhist and Taoist masters say that human beings naturally aspire to be happy, healthy, and at peace.

Through self-awareness, self-mastery, and being on purpose, I can choose my thoughts and therefore choose my vibration. When I find myself bothered or upset by another person or situation, I know that this is my signal to look inward, to reflect: *What is it that has caused me to attract this situation? To perceive this situation? To experience this situation? Is it a fear? Is it a belief? Or, Is it just what is?*

For example, I found myself bothered by someone who wanted to make sure that others were aware of his accomplishments. Upon self-reflection, I realized that I, too, wanted others to be aware of my accomplishments. I found myself bothered by someone who was wasting his time and not focused on what was clearly significant for him. When I looked within, I saw that I was wasting my time and not focusing on what was clearly significant for me. I found myself bothered by someone who verbally abused me. Upon self-reflection, I realized that I verbally abused myself all day long. I found myself being the victim of crimes—car thefts, a mugging, and break-ins—and realized that I had a fear of something violent happening to me. I lost money in a business transaction and realized that I didn't want the money. I believed that I didn't deserve to have wealth and that wealthy people aren't good people. I found myself being inappropriately harassed by certain people and discovered that I had done nothing except serve as a mirror for them. Rather than choosing to reflect, they chose to become angry.

Our thought patterns create our reality. At the outset of this book, I stated that the keys to success in work and life are, in fact, the same—those keys are self-awareness, self-mastery, and being on purpose. I said that in my own personal experience and from what I observed in others, without self-awareness, self-mastery, and being on purpose, we live each day as we did yesterday. We have the same experiences over and over again.

For what reason? After reading the previous chapters, you might say it's because our focus creates our reality. You might say that the focus causes a perception that then serves as the seed of an intention. This in turn affects our goals, which affects our actions, which creates the reality. And that is true—from the mind's perspective.

Biological science could add that as we think a thought, our bodies produce chemicals to which we can become addicted and then seek out a reality to satisfy these addictions. And that is true, too, from the body's perspective.

Quantum physics could add that we are all energy. We all vibrate according to the frequency of the vibration of our thought patterns. Like attracts like, and therefore like vibration attracts like vibration. Our thought patterns attract like thought patterns.

Our thought patterns attract like thought patterns.

terns. We think about pain and we attract pain. We think about peace and we attract peace. We think about failure and we attract failure. We think about thankfulness and we attract thankfulness.

From the spirit perspective, we have free will. With that free will we can choose to change the way we think. We can choose to change the way we vibrate. We can choose to break our addictions. We can choose to change our focus. We can choose our thought patterns. We can choose our reality.

Nothing we think, say, or do is trivial. Everything we think is a matter of choice. Everything we say or do is a matter of choice. Our circumstances, our destinies, and our successes are shaped by every choice we make.

It is amazing to think we have this power within us. We all do. It is our choice to access it. And

Everything we think is a matter of choice.

every moment presents a new opportunity to access that power, to shape our thoughts. There is no need to get angry or upset because you haven't accessed that power in the past. You've turned on the light. Enjoy the light. Take it from here.

SELF-MASTERY

One can have no smaller or greater mastery than the mastery of oneself.

—Leonardo da Vinci

To put the world right in order,
we must first put the nation in order;
to put the nation in order,
we must first put the family in order;
to put the family in order,
we must first cultivate our personal life . . .

—Confucius

16

DAILY CULTIVATION

W e have pruned and shaped our tree. We have decided what we want, determined what truly matters to us, and chosen our intentions. We have, through self-awareness, noticed the thoughts that are destructive and diseased—the thoughts that block our view of reality; waste our time, energy, and money; and move us away from our intentions. We have developed our powerful questions and powerful statements and have chosen to replace weak thought patterns with powerful thought patterns. So now what?

As gardeners, once we have pruned our tree, we pay attention to the daily cultivation of that tree—how it's watered, how it's fed, its environment, and its exposure to natural and unnatural elements. We take care in its daily cultivation so that the tree resists stress because we know that the trees that are susceptible to insects and disease are the trees that are stressed. With care in daily cultivation, the tree develops a strong root system, trunk, and branches and thrives in its full glory.

It's the same for us. We can pay attention to the daily cultivation of our mind, body, and spirit—how we think, how we're watered, how we're fed, our environment, and our exposure to natural and unnatural elements. We can take care in our daily cultivation so that we resist stress because we know that we are susceptible to disease and injury—physical and mental—when we are stressed. We know that with care in our daily cultivation, we thrive in our full glory.

We cultivate self-awareness, self-mastery, and being on purpose.

How do we cultivate ourselves? We cultivate our mind, body, and spirit. We cultivate ourselves in how we live our lives in each moment. We cultivate self-awareness. We cultivate self-mastery. We cultivate being on purpose. We manage our thought, we manage our energy, and we manage our spirit.

Cultivating ourselves is like a circular dance, and we can start anywhere in the circle. Some of you may choose to begin by cultivating your thoughts. This increases your energy, improves your life, improves your choices in eating, drinking, and exercising, and develops your spirit. Some of you may choose to cultivate your energy, which develops your spirit and helps you refine your thoughts and emotions. Some of you may choose to work on your spirit first, which favorably affects your thoughts and your energy. However you choose to start, just start.

In the following chapters, we look closely at managing our energy, managing our spirit, and managing our thoughts.

Choose your seeds. Plant the seeds. Cultivate.

Energy and persistence conquer all things.

—Benjamin Franklin

17

MANAGING ENERGY

We cultivate ourselves by managing our thoughts, managing our energy, and managing our spirit. Because it is a circular dance, managing our energy involves managing our mind, body, and spirit. Buddhists, Taoists, Hindus, and Native Americans all speak of the body being a temple and say that it is unnatural, and therefore sinful, to harm the body. They also speak of the importance of gathering and refining our energy to improve longevity, cultivate our minds, refine our emotions, and preserve our essence. (Those who follow the practices of ancient Chinese traditions believe that we are born with an original amount of energy called essence, and once the essence is depleted, our bodies die.) There are things we can do each day to increase and create a reserve of our energy, such as deep breathing, meditation, being thankful, and doing something we love. We can also do things that deplete our energy and reduce the reserve. If we don't deplete the reserve, we can preserve our essence and increase our longevity. If we do things that cause our

> *Managing energy involves managing mind, body, and spirit.*

reserve to drop into the negative, then we eat into our essence . . . until we die.

Our energy is affected, favorably or unfavorably, by what and how we choose to eat, drink, and breathe; how and how often we choose to exercise; what and how we choose to think; and what and how we choose to feel, say, and do.

Through the practice of self-awareness, we can renew our innate ability to be in tune with our energy, to know what increases and depletes our energy in each moment. We know what is good for us and what is not—physically, mentally, emotionally, and spiritually— in winter versus summer, in times

We can renew our innate ability to know what increases or depletes our energy.

of high physical activity versus low, in times of high mental activity versus low, in times of peace versus anxiety, in times of strength versus weakness, in times of health versus sickness. We know that what is good for everyone else is not necessarily good for us and what is good for us one day may not be good for us the next day.

Self-awareness is key. Self-mastery is key. Being on purpose is key. I invite you to choose to honor your body. The mind-body-spirit connection is very real. Can you remember a time when you felt in great physical condition? Didn't you feel happy? Focused? Energized? Powerful? Confident? Didn't things that might normally bother you simply roll off your shoulders? Weren't you able to think clearly?

I invite you to choose to manage your energy.

I used to believe that time was my most limited resource. I now know that energy is my most limited and most precious resource. When I find myself saying, *I don't have time for that,* I know that in most cases I am really saying that I don't have enough energy. I have heard others say, *I don't have enough time to spend with my kids or my spouse at night. When I get home from work, I just want to pass out on the couch.* That is an energy issue, not a time issue.

Extreme emotions, excess sensory input, taking action that is inconsistent with our values, excess desire, impatience, overstrain, overtiredness, ingesting the wrong drinks or foods, too much or too little exercise, the wrong kind of exercise, and seasonal changes all deplete our energy. Performing at our best also can deplete energy.

Most of us use up our energy resources and are forced into periods of low energy to rejuvenate. These low-energy periods can be negative if they take the form of burnout, hopelessness, or depression. We can also have positive low-energy periods if we take a restorative approach through taking a vacation, deep breathing, meditation, going for a walk, enjoying a hobby, listening to music, or sitting in the sauna. We can choose to take responsibility for our energy and choose to manage our energy to fulfill our intentions and achieve significant results.

ENERGY USERS

Overstrain

Impatience

Excess desire

Overtiredness

Extreme emotions

High performance

Seasonal changes

Excess sensory input

Physical overexertion

The wrong kind of exercise

Too much or too little sleep

Too much or too little exercise

Inability to digest foods efficiently

Acting inconsistently with our values

Ingesting drinks or foods that harm the body

In Chapter 12, I wrote about the time I almost lost my eyesight from dehydration. I also weighed thirty pounds more than I do today. I had sinus infections, migraines, broken teeth and nails, kidney infections, and bad colds on a regular basis. Since 1998, I haven't experienced any of these problems.

I used to think my body was a nuisance—I constantly told myself that I did not have time to eat, sleep, rest, or go on vacation to rejuvenate. When I decided to choose to be thankful for my body and the strength and nourishment of my food and drink, honor my body, guard my thoughts, and look forward to being of service, my health and energy changed dramatically for the better.

A few small changes can dramatically increase your energy and performance.

Now, you might be thinking, *Oh, God, please don't ask me to change what I am eating. And please don't ask me to exercise.* I'm not. I am inviting you to take responsibility for your energy. As with your thoughts, you can choose to manage your energy. I am inviting you to be aware of your energy users. Notice what crosses your lips during a day and whether it increases or depletes your energy.

I invite you to be mindful of your intentions with respect to your energy and to be mindful of the choices you make throughout the day that affect your energy. A few small changes can dramatically increase your energy and performance. These changes don't involve changing what you eat. They involve managing your thoughts. Ironically, you could eat the healthiest food in the world and it could have no impact whatsoever. It could even have a negative impact. How you eat your food and what you are thinking as you eat your food significantly affect the results you get from eating and your performance throughout the day. Thoughts such as worry, anger, guilt, anxiety, feeling overwhelmed, sadness, and disappointment negatively affect how your body processes food. Similarly, peaceful, happy, caring, loving, and thankful thoughts can powerfully affect the energy you gain from your food and exercise.

Here are five rules of thumb to consider in managing your energy:

MANAGING ENERGY

Five Rules of Thumb

1. Cultivate the spirit of health and vitality.
2. Choose your intentions and remind yourself of them.
3. Be mindful of the matter at hand.
4. Take the time to rejuvenate.
5. Breathe deeply.

---

1. Cultivate the spirit of health and vitality.

Recapture your state of wonder and develop an endless appreciation for the amazing functions and capabilities of your body. If you are in pain, marvel at your body's ability to signal that something is wrong and requires care and attention. If you are injured, appreciate and call upon the body's amazing ability to heal. If you are taking a walk, be thankful for your brain and your nervous and musculature systems that make it possible to do so. If you are in ill health, be thankful for all that is healthy and working. Be thankful for the cleansing that is taking place now. Contemplate, in a wondrous way, what you can do or how you might be able to effect healing. Quiet yourself and hear your answers. Cultivate your health and vitality.

2. Choose your intentions and remind yourself of them.

What we focus on creates our reality, so watch your thoughts. *I shouldn't be eating this. This is so bad for me. I can't relax. This is not fun. I can't do this for twenty minutes.* If you are thinking any of these thoughts, you are focusing on and creating the very reality you don't want.

Before you eat your meal or begin to exercise, exhale deeply, then inhale, and choose your intention. What is the result you intend? To be strengthened and nourished? Revitalized? Healed? Detoxified? Reenergized? Relaxed? Recentered?

What good arises from the fulfillment of your intention? The energy to enjoy the evening with your family? The ability to center yourself in order to guide and mentor others? The health and longevity to be a vital part of your grandchildren's lives? The clarity to be fully present?

3. Be mindful of the matter at hand.

We all know that when we focus on a job, it gets done. We all know that when we don't focus on a job, it never gets done or gets done less than optimally. This is equally true when it comes to managing energy. For me, I sleep well, wake up refreshed, require less sleep, am calm, make great decisions, have fun, and am compassionate and effective when I am healthy. From a time-management and return-on-investment perspective, it makes sense to me to choose to invest time to cultivate my health.

Consider taking time to eat your meals or snacks without doing other things. In most cases, we are better off not to eat a meal than to eat a meal while watching television, reading a book, driving, or running out the door. Denny Waxman, the founder and director of the Strengthening Health Institute in Philadelphia, PA, says that his students ask why it isn't good to eat on the go or while doing something else. His response: "How about I watch TV or read a book right now during your consultation? Wait just a minute. I've got to see this. Oh, excuse me. What did you just say?"

How would you feel? I would feel like Denny wasn't paying attention to me. I would feel like I wasn't receiving the full benefit of his consultation. I might even feel like I was getting no benefit.

It is the same for our bodies. We have a powerful impact on our bodies and their ability to process food and to heal. When we do not take the time to allow ourselves to focus on eating, strengthening, and nourishing our bodies, We do not receive the full benefit of the meal. Worse, if we are focusing on negative thoughts and activities instead of enjoying a quiet meal, our bodies are not able to process the meal at all. We get tired in the afternoon, we don't think clearly, we need antacids, we have irregular or painful bowel movements, and we don't sleep well. We waste far more time being unproductive, going to the doctor, or being sick than we would have spent taking the time to focus on increasing our energy.

Even worse, we do not allow our minds to be quiet, so we are oblivious to our higher awareness—the higher awareness that knows when we have eaten enough and that signals us about what foods are best to eat right now to heal ourselves or maximize our health and longevity.

Our thoughts affect the body's ability to process food and to heal.

This is the same higher awareness that knows which type of exercise is best for us. If we pay attention, we notice which foods energize us and which ones make us lethargic, which foods warm us and which ones cool us, which foods nourish us and which ones are harmful.

When I started taking the time to relax and enjoy my meals, I found many thoughts racing through my head. Many of them were thoughts I didn't want to face or deal with. It was very tempting to turn on the TV, read, or do something else to distract myself and avoid the issue. With practice, it became easier and easier to eat quietly without doing other things and without talking about what went wrong during the day. Now I find it irritating to have the TV on. My thoughts have cleared, and I have become open to my higher awareness. I have discovered through my higher awareness to avoid milk in my coffee or drinking milk and orange juice during the same meal. I discovered that I had been sick to my stomach for years and didn't even know it. Later I was guided to avoid drinking coffee and caffeinated beverages. I was guided to organic whole foods and seaweed.

Just as we require a certain amount of sleep each night to heal and rejuvenate our minds and bodies, we require regular meals and a certain amount of time to eat. I invite you to take twenty minutes for each meal. Focus on relaxing your mind and body, chew well, receive nourishment, and increase your energy. If you want to start with baby steps, try taking twenty minutes with just one meal a day for thirty days or all three meals for just one day a week. Notice how you feel. Then go for two meals or two days. Similarly, focus on and devote at least twenty minutes to exercise, deep breathing, or whatever you are doing to increase your energy.

4. Take the time to rejuvenate.

Catherine McCarthy, Ph.D., coauthor of *Leading at the Edge* and a principal of The Energy Project, teaches that we can approach the management of our energy as if we were a sprinter and not a marathoner. The key is to rejuvenate, and it's the quality of the rejuvenation, not the quantity, that matters. She teaches that when we are in high-energy situations, we need only thirty seconds of high-quality rejuvenation every ninety minutes. That is a very high return on investment and worth seeing for yourself. Through self-awareness, you know how much rejuvenation you may

We need only thirty seconds of high-quality rejuvenation every ninety minutes.

need, depending on whether you are utilizing physical, mental, emotional, or spiritual energy. For example, you may want to breathe deeply, stretch, listen to certain music, drink some water, call someone, look at your family photos, go for a walk, commune with nature, or remind yourself of your intentions. Or you may want to exercise, sleep, or change your diet. When you pay attention, you are aware of what you need to rejuvenate.

5. Breathe deeply.

How we breathe is critical to vibrant health and energy. Breathing controls the condition of the bloodstream. It controls the flow of lymph and stimulates the body's immune system. We inhale fresh air and exhale toxins that have accumulated in the body. How

Deep breathing dramatically increases our energy.

we breathe also has a profound effect on our nervous systems. Metaphysically, deep breathing dramatically increases our energy and is highly effective in releasing negative emotions and forceful and weak thought patterns. Those who have taken Lamaze childbirth classes or participated in natural childbirth understand the significance of breathing.

The way I hold myself, the way I breathe, and the way I move all affect my mindset, attitude, and ability to relax, think clearly, take in life fully, and enjoy myself. If your breaths are short or if you notice that your shoulders and neck tighten when you breathe, you are contributing to your own anxiety and ill health.

I use a simple technique. I sit or stand with my spine straight and my feet placed shoulder width apart. I exhale deeply for six counts. Then I hold my breath for three counts. I then inhale deeply for six counts to fully expand my diaphragm. I hold my breath for three counts. I exhale deeply for six counts and wait for three counts, until I inhale again. I do this at least three times. If you are weak and need strength, focus on your inhalation and inhale first. If you want to calm yourself or shift your thinking, focus on your exhalation and exhale first. When we practice this breathing technique in *Managing Thought* workshops, the participants remark how much better they feel—in less than one minute. I admit that it has sometimes taken as many as eighteen deep breaths, focusing on my exhalation, to release my anger. It's amazing, though, to be able to release anger in less than three minutes and in so doing prevent the negative effect on my body from thinking angry thoughts.

Focusing on our breath before we say or do something is very powerful. You've heard the saying "Take a deep breath." Taking

> *Focusing on our breath before we say or do something gives us the moment to be mindful.*

that breath gives us the moment to be mindful—to gather our thoughts, recenter, add light to situations, see if what we are about to do or say is consistent with our vision and values, and choose our intentions. I invite you to pay attention to your breathing, choose to breathe deeply, and take in life fully.

*He who rules his spirit
has won a greater victory
than the taking of a city.*

—Jesus

18

MANAGING SPIRIT

Through shaping our thoughts, lifting them higher each day, and focusing our thoughts, intentions, and actions on what serves our purpose, we develop our spirit. By developing our higher awareness and increasing our level of consciousness and energy, we also develop our spirit. Here are three rules of thumb to develop our spirit and make it soar.

DEVELOPING SPIRIT AND MAKING IT SOAR

Three Rules of Thumb

1. Be of service.
2. Be thankful.
3. Be quiet each day.

---

1. Be of service.

In Chapter 13, I wrote about the tremendous power of asking the question *How can I be of service?* When we ask this question, we automatically shift to a higher level of thinking. Our focus turns from taking something personally or seeking to be understood to a focus on learning, wonder, possibility, and seeking to understand. Asking how we can be of service replaces stress with caring (which leads to good health, as we learned earlier). Asking how we can be of service brings about

> *When we are being of service, we are in a powerful state.*

rich rewards: prosperity, satisfaction, happiness, and inner peace. When we are being of service, we are in a powerful state.

We make a difference. We achieve greatness.

When we are being of service, we vibrate at a high level and attract to us people and situations that vibrate at high levels. This is why it is powerful, when we choose and develop our intentions, to sincerely intend what good comes from the fulfillment of our intentions.

Earlier, I discussed how I was frustrated because I really wanted to make a difference and I questioned whether my job, my career path, or the widgets manufactured by the company I was involved with made a difference. I remember discovering that I held a limiting belief that I could not be a successful businessperson and live a life of service. I also believed that I could not be a prosperous person and live a life of service. Since living a life of service is my life mission and being a successful businessperson is also a priority for me, I was stuck by seemingly conflicting purposes and values. Although I earned a comfortable salary, I found myself in debt and, quite frankly, the busiest person in the poorhouse. I then realized I held another limiting belief with respect to my definition of living a life of service. What kind of person did I think I had to be to dedicate myself to a life of service? Mother Teresa? Or a CEO? It was a big *aha!* for me to realize that I could live a life of service in each moment, no matter what I was doing. I could live a life of service as a CEO, teacher, daughter, sister, mentor, or team player. We can make a difference in any moment of work and life.

When we quiet ourselves and then ask how we can be of service, we may discover that we are already of tremendous service. This discovery gives rise to a new per-

> *We can make a difference in any moment of work and life.*

spective that results in satisfaction, happiness, and inner peace. We become inspired, rise to an even higher level, and then inspire others.

A friend of mine was unhappy because he felt that his work lacked purpose. I asked him what he did with the money he made from his work. When we followed the path of the money, he found significant purpose. His son went to a fine school dedicated to developing fine human beings, which was of service to his son and to his son's future spouse, children, employer, and colleagues. His ex-wife was using alimony to educate herself and work toward the fulfillment of her dreams, which was of service to their son and to all with whom she comes into contact. He contributed to some excellent organizations that made a difference for humankind, and his purchases supported the livelihoods of many. Many people were benefitted through the use of the money he earned.

I've always remembered the story of a young man who went to work in an orange juice factory. As the new man on the job, he was assigned to what he felt was one of the lowest assignments— packing the orange juice cartons into crates. He spent each day watching the clock, looking forward to going home. One day, he was partnered with an old-timer who had been working there for years. He felt disrespect for the older man for not being inspired to do something other than pack crates. As they were working, he learned a valuable lesson. He noticed that while he worked with this old-timer, he didn't watch the clock and the day just flew by. This man, he observed, didn't just pack crates, he carefully packed crates and announced, "Oh! Be careful with that one, that's going to a family in Tennessee" and "Oooh, let's make sure that's right for that little boy in Philadelphia." This man had purpose. He was joyful. He was inspiring.

One of my clients, Maureen Gallagher, is well known in the worker's compensation insurance field. She has developed programs for her clients that show how being of service to their workforce as part of their everyday culture dramatically reduces the number and amount of claims, as well as premiums.

Maureen has taken being of service to another level by sharing these programs with other agents—her competitors—and developing certification programs. There are many who ask her why she doesn't keep her programs a secret and retain a competitive advantage. It is Maureen's intention to transform the landscape of worker's compensation, reduce injury, and give employers an incentive to develop a good working culture. She is working for the greater good. Furthermore, she has found that her business has grown substantially, and continues to grow substantially, by providing this service. She has gained business from training her competitors and has won many new clients because of her recognized expertise.

A note of caution: There is a big difference between being of service and being a doormat. One is powerful; the other is weak. Through self-awareness, you know the difference. Being of service should not cause you harm. Being of service to yourself is the greatest gift you can give to yourself, your family, your organization, and humanity.

We are of service when we utilize our gifts and talents.

Being of highest and best service is made possible when we are being true to ourselves and utilizing our gifts and talents. Then we find ourselves to be in flow, in the moment, fully present, oblivious to the passage of time, and in a state of joy and happiness.

When we are clear in our intentions and sincere in wanting to be of service, doors open for us (or perhaps we can see the doors that were open all along), and we can walk through those open doors filled with faith and gratitude.

2. Be thankful.

The simple act of being thankful takes us to a new level of awareness, vision, and creativity for ourselves, our families, and our organizations. When we think thoughts of thankfulness, purpose, and wonder, we learn quickly, the creative regions of our brains light up, our creative juices flow, and our bodies produce chemicals that boost our health and vitality. We became inspired. We begin to glow. We become in tune with our higher awareness. When we are focused on being thankful, we perceive even more that makes us thankful. We live a joyous self-fulfilling prophecy.

When we are focused on being thankful, we perceive even more that makes us thankful.

Have you noticed that the people who are consistently happy are the one's who are most appreciative of even the smallest of things? Have you noticed that you enjoy giving to people who are truly thankful and that you may stop giving to people who don't show any appreciation? Our spirit works in much the same way. Our spirits are lifted when we are appreciative of even the smallest things. When we express thanks for a compliment and appreciate ourselves for the progress we are making as we cultivate ourselves, our spirits soar, we experience joy, and we want to do more.

If we have contempt or hate for anything we wish to change, we will not be able to change it. If we hate our relationships, we will remain trapped in those relationships or will experience the same type of relationships over and over again. If we hate our business, we will remain trapped in that business. If instead we can be thankful and appreciative of what we have, we open ourselves to receive more of what we want.

> *Our spirits are lifted when we are appreciative of even the smallest things.*

The Taoist Master Om Ni Hua Ching (affectionately known as Om Ni) and founder of Yo San University in Santa Monica, CA, likens this to a filled bucket. If we do not empty the bucket, we cannot receive more. Until we say thank you—the equivalent of pouring out what is in the bucket—we are unable to receive fresh water. We remain forever burdened with whatever is in the bucket, which becomes stagnant and laden with bacteria and algae.

I often work with managers who feel down about everything—the industry, employees, suppliers, investors, and customers. I ask them to list everything they have to be thankful for with respect to these things.

As they prepare the list, a transformation occurs. Their faces light up, their postures straighten, they begin to smile, and their creative juices begin to flow. They begin to ask questions. *What can we do to attract more customers like Customer A? What can we do to have more employees like Jake, Susan, and David? How can we help more suppliers perform like Supplier B?* They begin to formulate a vision and see the possibility of greatness. I see them recapture their power and begin to have fun.

I invite you to cultivate thinking about what you are thankful for. Do this before beginning a conversation or meeting, at the end of a conversation or meeting, at the beginning and end of the workday and the day. If you suffer from scarcity of time, be thankful for the time you *do* have and for each experience you are having. If you were to implement *just one thing,* it could be the practice of being thankful. You will see a dramatic improvement in your relationships, in your creativity, in your spirit, and in your life.

3. Be quiet each day.

Throughout the book, I have mentioned the significance of taking the time to be quiet each day—to cleanse and open your mind to

Being quiet each day cleanses and opens our minds to our higher awareness.

your higher awareness, know the right thing to do, access ideas, and spark your creativity. We have the ability to quiet ourselves to discover the essence of our desires, fears, obstacles, and limiting beliefs. We have the ability to ask ourselves questions and listen for the answers. We have the ability to remind ourselves of our intentions and be self-aware in each moment.

I believe that many of us are in grave danger of losing our spirit. Few of us are mindful of how we are really living. We are claimed and absorbed by our work and day-to-day activities. We seek excitement in sports or news. We stimulate our nerves through movies, television, music, and fiction. We may even seek the thrill of spirituality and mysticism.

To relax, we distract ourselves. We do not rest. We do not cleanse. We do not tap into the tremendous power of our higher awareness. Each day, we require more and more distraction. We become diverted from our true nature and our purpose in living. We look outside ourselves for answers and solutions to our dilemmas of mind, body, and spirit. Instead, we can follow the advice printed on a bumper sticker I saw: "Don't just do something—sit there!"

Robert Nourse, the founder of Vistage International, also known as TEC, the preeminent organization for the professional and personal development of CEOs, said it best when he said, "I want to keep the channels open." He was referring to clearing his mind and body of distractions and being open and fully receptive to his higher awareness. When our channels are open, our minds are clear, the world changes, and remarkable things start to happen. We all have the ability to keep our channels open.

> *When we quiet ourselves, our channels are open, and remarkable things start to happen.*

Many of us take the time to wash ourselves and brush our teeth to remove the dirt and grime that builds up each day. We don't give it a second thought. Yet we go days, weeks, even years, without taking a shower for our brains. Dirt and grime build up each day, clouding our windshield and adding more layers to our onion.

I hear many different excuses. *I don't have time. I can't sit still. I can't relax. I am too busy.* Ironically, if you took a moment to quiet yourself, you could know that your excuses are symptoms of not taking the time to be quiet each day. What is the essence of your excuse?

Although my excuses were being too busy and not having the time, the essence of my excuses was fear. I knew that when I was truly alone with myself I could discover what I could be and ought to be and was not. I knew that I could discover how far removed I was from my higher

> *Nothing is more certain of reward than the cultivation of the power within.*

awareness and from my own divinity. I knew that I could see how much difficulty my spirit was having in living in the world I had created and that my whole life was a struggle against this truth. I knew that in my body and soul I could discover a power of another kind. I could be transformed. I was frightened of transformation, the not knowing what could become of me—the *me* I had artificially created and presented to the world as my identity.

There is tremendous power in taking the time to be quiet each day. Nothing is more certain of reward than the cultivation of the power within. James Allen, author of *As a Man Thinketh*, said, "The more tranquil we become, the greater our success, our influence, our power for good."

If you were to choose *just one thing* from this book, taking the time to quiet yourself brings about significant transformation. If you have not practiced quieting yourself before, then do so for 30 seconds. Then go for a minute, then two minutes, and so on until you can do so for 20 minutes. There are many ways you may choose to quiet yourself. Through self-awareness, you know when you are quieting yourself versus distracting yourself.

Certainly, doing deep-breathing exercises, walking barefoot in the grass, communing with nature, exercising, performing yoga, sitting quietly, and enjoying a massage or hot bath is relaxing and does wonders for washing away the thoughts and emotions that lie on the surface. Creative ideas emerge when you give your mind a rest. Regular practice of any one of these quieting techniques can have a significant impact on your daily life, work, creativity, and emotional balance.

> *Through self-awareness, we are quieting ourselves versus distracting ourselves.*

This only scratches the surface. We all have the ability to go even deeper, through meditation, to connect with our higher awareness and achieve our highest potential.

Perhaps you have tried meditation and stopped because too many thoughts kept coming and you weren't able to achieve "no thoughts." Please know that this is what happens during meditation. Thoughts rise to the surface to be washed away, just as dirt loosens and is rinsed away when we bathe.

According to Eknath Easwaran, whom many consider the best meditation teacher of our times, when we quiet ourselves through meditation, "We take hold of and concentrate to the utmost degree our latent mental power. It consists in training the mind, especially attention and the will, so that we can set forth from the surface level of consciousness and journey into the very depths." Through meditation, we find within ourselves a power that can indeed transform us.

I invite you to take a step toward managing your spirit and notice the transformation that begins to occur in your work and life by being of service, being thankful, and taking the time to quiet yourself.

Thinking is easy, acting is difficult, and to put one's thoughts into action is the most difficult thing in the world.

—Goethe

19

MANAGING THOUGHT: PUTTING IT INTO PRACTICE

It is key to remember that everything we think, say, and do first begins in thought. So to begin anywhere in the circular dance of mind, body, and spirit actually requires thought. Ideas, attitude, desires, beliefs, intentions, passion, planning, choosing to take action, being thankful, and acknowledging or celebrating progress are all

With practice, your new way of thinking becomes natural for you.

thoughts. *Managing Thought* comes into play in every aspect of self-cultivation. We choose our desires, beliefs, intentions, powerful questions, and powerful statements. We choose to practice, take action, observe, and reflect; and we choose self-awareness.

Managing Thought takes practice, and as we talked about earlier, practice makes permanent. Mark Twain once said he practiced six weeks for an impromptu speech. With practice, your new way of thinking becomes natural for you. Through practice—through watchfulness, patience, and self-control in each moment—you can change the way you think. You can change your nature. You can transform your life.

Practicing *Managing Thought* can be hard to do in the heat of the moment. Our brains go into action and present us with fight, flight, and freeze thoughts practically instantaneously, followed very quickly by the series of fight, flight, and freeze thoughts

Begin by practicing self-awareness when you are alone.

we have been practicing for years. For this reason, it's not necessary or even advisable to begin your practice while you're in the middle of a difficult situation or dealing with a difficult person. Dave Hopla, professional basketball shooting coach, teaches his students to first practice the shots closest to the basket. After they master the close shots and have gained confidence, they practice shooting from farther and farther away. Only after these shots are mastered does he teach his students to shoot against an opposing player.

First practice by yourself the shots closest to the basket. Begin by practicing self-awareness—by watching your thoughts when you are alone. You will find that you are alone with your thoughts often throughout the day: while you are driving, in the bathroom, getting ready for bed, on hold on the phone, walking from the car to your destination, exercising, and eating, for example.

Practice noticing your thoughts as an observer, without blame or judgment. Practice looking *at* your thoughts instead of *from* your thoughts. Practice noticing whether you are buying into your thoughts. Practice noticing what

Practice looking **at** *your thoughts instead of* **from** *them.*

choices you are making as a result of your thoughts. Practice
noticing whether these choices
serve your purpose. Practice no-

Practice breathing deeply and restating your intentions.

ticing patterns of thought. As an unbiased observer, practice
choosing how you might think or react differently the next time
a similar situation arises.

Practice breathing, exhaling deeply, smiling, and restating your
intentions—first thing in the morning and last thing at night. Before
you start your day or before you go into a difficult situation, practice
taking a deep breath, exhaling deeply, smiling, asking yourself
powerful questions, and restating your powerful statements and
intentions. Then practice managing your thoughts and reactions
while you're in the middle of a situation and experiencing the
interaction. Practice letting go of
habitual thoughts and replacing
them with new thoughts. Notice
how long you are able to think

Practice transforming thoughts that carry blame and judgment.

these new thoughts before reverting back to the old thought patterns.
Notice the thought you had when you chose to revert back to your
habitual thoughts and behavior. See the essence of that thought. Ask
yourself if it is true. Ask yourself if you can think of any reason to
keep that thought. Ask yourself if this thought is serving you.

Choose your intention for the next time. (All this can be done
very quickly once you have developed the practice of self-awareness and self-mastery.)

Practice this technique during a conversation with someone. Notice which thoughts are pertinent to the matter at hand.
Notice which thoughts carry blame and judgment. Notice which
thoughts are focused on you and what you are feeling and what
you are going to say next. Practice listening to others, keeping

the focus off yourself, and letting go of thoughts that aren't pertinent to the conversation. Practice transforming the thoughts that carry blame and judgment into caring, clarifying questions. Notice the impact that your listening has on the person.

You may find that as you enter into certain situations with family members, employees, or coworkers, for example, old, familiar patterns of thinking and reacting emerge. Even though your intention is to think and react a certain way, you find yourself reverting to an old dynamic just as if you were on autopilot and not able to manage your thoughts at all. This is because you have wired your brain to look for, focus on, see, and react to things in a certain way. The more you have thought, felt, and acted this way in the past, the stronger that wiring has become. It is no wonder that you fall into old familiar patterns.

When you find yourself reverting to an old thought pattern, do a *do-over*.

One fun and effective thing I have resurrected from my childhood that helps rewire my neural nets is the *do-over*. For example, let's say my intention is to serve as a guide and mentor to an associate and I find myself criticizing the associate and telling him or her what to do. I can stop myself midstream or go back later and tell the associate I want a *do-over*. I then leave the room and come back in, greet the associate, and redo the whole conversation. This works particularly well with spouses, kids, customers, and coworkers. Have fun with it. You'll find the other person feels valued and appreciated because you are genuine in what you think, say, and do.

Another way to cultivate managing your thoughts is to practice *just one thing* each day.

PRACTICE *JUST ONE THING* EACH DAY

- Notice my thoughts and feelings
- Notice when I am in fight, flight, or freeze and add light to the situation
- Invoke the state of wonder
- Change *You* to *I*
- Change *But* to *And*
- Change *Need To* or *Have To* to *Choose*
- Change *Should* to *Could*
- Focus on what I want
- Determine the essence of what I want
- Create my intention
- Seek to understand
- Practice being thankful
- Stay in the moment
- Breathe
- Practice do-overs
- Eat mindfully

If you can practice any one of these each day, even for just ten seconds more each day, you are taking an immeasurable step toward self-awareness, self-mastery, and being on purpose.

If you believe you can't do it, try putting a new slide in your View-Master that says that you can or wonder what the one thing is that you could practice. It's possible for all of us to reinvent ourselves and achieve new levels of consciousness. Believing that you can't manage your thoughts or that it's difficult is a limiting belief. Try on a new belief.

Practice makes permanent.

Is it your intention to overcome your own programming? Is it your intention to live the life you intend? To be happy and at peace? To make a difference? To be of highest and best service?

We know that practice makes permanent.

We know that we are capable of reinventing ourselves, of unraveling and rewiring our own neural nets. It takes practice, repetition, self-awareness, and self-mastery. It takes making note of our performance, without blame or judgment, and quickly adjusting what we say, what we do, and how we react, honing and polishing ourselves. In time, we notice that we have changed, that we are no longer thinking certain thoughts or that it's the normal course of business for us to ask an empowering question or choose our intentions.

I remember a study that examined high-performing athletes to see what behaviors made them so great. Larry Bird is one example. Besides his passion for basketball, his behavior illuminates the significance of practice, making note of performance, and making adjustments without blame or judgment.

What distinguished Bird was self-awareness. When he watched a game film, he watched the game film. While his teammates laughed and ribbed each other, he was focused on the game film. What distinguished Bird was self-mastery. Before every game, he was practicing, honing his skills, long before his teammates arrived. What distinguished Bird was his ability to be on purpose, observing his performance without blame or judgment, immediately making note of adjustments he could make and then making the adjustments on his next shots. Others, when they missed a shot, blamed their health, their mood, the

Reflection is a very powerful action.

fans, the noise, the floor, and so forth, and did not adjust their behavior.

It may be helpful to note that *reflection is an action,* a very powerful action. Taking a moment to reflect on our successes and failures brings invaluable learning and opportunity for growth. We can simply ask ourselves these questions: *What can I learn from this? How can I change? What can I do differently the next time?*

As we practice managing our thoughts, many of our counterproductive thoughts go away. Will they go away permanently? Will your brain never again present you with a doubt thought or a worry thought or a fear thought or any other fight, flight, or freeze thought? I do not know the answer. I know that I am human and have counterproductive thoughts. I also know that although no life is free from troubles, our minds can be trouble-free when we practice self-awareness, self-mastery, and being on purpose. Significant results depend on how quickly you observe that you are having a thought, how quickly you determine whether the thought is serving your purpose, how quickly you choose whether to let the thought rule your world, how quickly you choose what action to take, and how quickly you take that action—all in a state of thankfulness and wonder.

Some food for thought: As you practice *Managing Thought*, you may encounter some challenges as you find the story you've created for yourself changing. I discussed noticing your story in Chapter 10 in the context of identifying limiting beliefs. To illustrate the challenge, I share my own story.

For most of my work career, I had developed a personal and professional story of being important, being needed, and, as a result, being very busy. If I took a vacation, I scheduled my activities around making and receiving phone calls and faxes and preparing and receiving documents for overnight express. If others wished me a great vacation, I made sure to tell them that I would be working and was reachable if they needed me. If anyone asked me how I enjoyed my vacation, I made sure they knew that I worked most of the time. When I changed my thoughts, and ultimately my way of being, to value my vacation time—to relax, rejuvenate, and be of service (instead of being needed and important)—I found it difficult to tell my new story. I discovered that my identity was all wrapped up in my old story. I discovered that I was uncomfortable creating a new identity. I had thoughts of fear of what others might think of the new identity. I also found it to be very much a habit to tell others and myself how busy I was. It took a conscious effort for me to share with others how much I looked forward to the vacation and how much I was enjoying my vacation or had enjoyed my vacation. With practice, enjoying my vacation has become natural for me. With practice, not worrying about what others might think has become natural for me. Not having an identity has become natural for me (although this is a work in progress).

At a *Managing Thought* workshop, a woman revealed that she was unable to concentrate on the topic at hand because she had so much going wrong in her life. She then proceeded to tell me about what was going wrong with her sister, her mother, and her neighbor. There wasn't anything wrong with *her* life. When she changes her slide in her View-Master, she may find it difficult to project a new story when asked, *How are you?* She may want to practice answering, *Wonderful!* With self-awareness and practice, she will be able to separate her own well-being from those of others, be thankful for her well-being, and determine how she can be of service to help her friends and family.

> *In periods of low energy, old, negative, weak thinking rises to the surface to be washed away.*

More food for thought: As you practice *Managing Thought*, you may find that long-gone thoughts are reappearing. In periods of low energy and low thought patterns, our lower awareness often emerges and old, negative, weak thought patterns resurface. They can be the result of a previous tendency of fight, flight, or freeze. They can be the result of conclusions you've drawn about similar experiences or habits you've developed in dealing with past circumstances.

When these weak and negative thoughts reappear, they can be frightening. You may ask yourself, *Why are they back? I thought this was long gone, not a part of my nature anymore?* The key observation and reminder is that the reappearance of these thoughts is in fact a form of detoxification—

> *In choosing our intentions, we break down old thought patterns and build new ones.*

a purification of your thinking. Old, negative, weak thinking stored in your brain from past experiences is rising to the surface to be washed away. The fact that you are observing the thought and not *unconsciously* surrendering to it is indicative of the growth you have achieved. In choosing your intentions, you forge a higher course of thinking and action. You break down old patterns and build new ones. The initial fright, the purification, the acknowledgment of growth, and the building of new, powerful patterns can all be acknowledged and celebrated.

When we practice self-awareness, even in difficult times, we can see these thoughts for what they are—thoughts. We know that we are the observer of these thoughts, and we can choose whether to utilize them. We can choose our intentions.

As you practice *Managing Thought*, you may become bombarded with an overwhelming number of weak, negative, nonconstructive thoughts. This reminds me of the turkey pan we clean at Thanksgiving. First we soak the pan. Then we start to clean the pan, and as we do, the pan seems to get dirtier and dirtier while we scrub and loosen all that was stuck to it. Then, suddenly, the pan is clean. As we practice *Managing Thought* and begin to unravel a

The more often we practice in a state of openness, receptivity, thankfulness, and wonder, the sooner the result comes.

pattern of thinking, the inter-related patterns may begin to unravel as well. The good news is that this creates a step-function increase in the power of your thinking. Remember, your progress is logarithmic, not linear. You will experience some gradual change, and you will also experience a transformation as you rise to a new level of thinking.

The more often we practice, the sooner the result comes. The more often we practice in a state of openness and receptivity (without blame or judgment), the sooner the result comes. The more thankful and curious we are as we practice, the sooner the result comes.

I am willing to change my thoughts.

I change my thoughts easily and effortlessly.

I value change. I make my choices in service of change.

I am thankful for the ability to change my thoughts.

We can begin to manage our thoughts with the little things—how we choose to think and react in a traffic jam, while we're standing in a long line, when an employee or loved one makes a mistake, when a customer makes a demand, when an investor or a relative makes a comment, when our partners are cranky, or when the kids are screaming—the choices we make in the day-to-day moments of our lives.

My capacity to understand, accept, forgive, be on purpose, abide by my values and principles, keep my mind free of all the chatter, eat healthy foods, exercise, breathe deeply, and be thankful contributes to the daily cultivation of my personal power, the continuous improvement of myself. It's easy to cultivate ourselves if we're meditating at the top of a mountain or in a cave somewhere away from the day-to-day hassles of life. True self-cultivation develops by applying ourselves in our daily lives.

However you choose to start, just start. Like a one-year-old learning to walk, take the first step. Celebrate. Take another step. Or be outrageous and take lots of steps. Fall. Get back up, take a deep breath, and take another step. There is an old Chinese proverb that says, "Be not afraid of growing slowly, be afraid only of standing still." So make small changes, enjoy the results, and build momentum as you transform your life.

*The journey
of a thousand miles
begins with
a single step.*

—Lao-Tzu

20

ENJOY THE JOURNEY

M*anaging Thought* is not a quick fix. It is a labor of love, a sacred quest. It is the best gift you can give to yourself, your family, your organization, and the world. I hope you can see that *Managing Thought* is a journey, a *continuous* process. Can you experience the joy of the process?

> **Managing Thought** *is a continuous process.*

Many of us—executives in particular—don't have much patience for process. We want results, and we do not allow ourselves to be happy until we feel we have achieved the goal. When I compliment people or congratulate them on an accomplishment, I have found that most people do not say, *Thank you.* Instead they say, *Yes, but I still have this and that left to do.* I was like that, too, until I had an *aha!*

I realized that one of the great qualities of human beings is that we are expansive. It is our nature. When we are expansive, we naturally seek ways to become better, so we set goals. What do we do when the accomplishment of a goal is in sight? Because we are expansive, we set a new goal. I realized that if I do not allow myself to be happy until a goal is achieved, and my goals are always overlapping, I will never be happy.

I then realized that the real joy is in being true to my nature, in being expansive. With that realization, I can smile and say, *Thank you*, and I can notice and acknowledge or celebrate each step in my continuing process of expansion. I can acknowledge how far I have come *and* reaffirm my commitment to expansion.

With each step, acknowledge or celebrate your victory. Celebrate your humanity. Celebrate your self-awareness. And no matter how small, even if it was nine seconds in a thirty-minute situation, celebrate your self-mastery and your ability to choose your thoughts. Next time, go for twenty seconds, a minute, two minutes, ten minutes, and so on, until it becomes natural for you.

Celebrate your victory, your humanity, and your self-awareness.

Be thankful that you have the ability to choose your thoughts. In a happy, celebratory, and wondrous way, take note of what you can do differently next time.

When we experience the joy of the process and acknowledge and celebrate every change we make, no matter how small, we achieve significant results.

We can see how this works when we're participating in the transformation of a one-year-old who is learning to walk. We watch carefully for some small movement that looks like a step. We cheer wildly and encourage the child to try it again, to take another step, then another. We hug and kiss the child and joyously celebrate as the child transforms.

What if we punished or berated the child who hadn't taken that first step, or whose first step was wobbly, or who had momentarily gone back to crawling? What if, after that first step, we demanded that the child run? How quickly would the child have walked?

It's the same for us. We learn quickly, we're creative, and we are inspired when we're in a state of joy and thankfulness. So watch yourself and remember that if you have become aware of your thoughts—that's a win. If you notice a thought that is unconstructive—that's a win.

We are inspired when we are in a state of joy and thankfulness.

If you have the intent to change that thought—that's a win. If you're able to change how you think after you have observed an unconstructive thought—that's a win. If, when you are dealing with a difficult person or a difficult situation and you are able to think differently for only nine seconds—that, too, is a win. The next day, go for fifteen seconds, then thirty, then fifteen minutes, until you have changed your nature and your new way of thinking is natural for you.

As you practice *Managing Thought*, you will find that like the tree that has been pruned, shaped, and daily cultivated, you will thrive. When we are thriving, we feel free. We are confident and at peace. We love ourselves. We love what we do. We have loving relationships at work and at home. We are open and receptive. We are expansive and creative. We are engaged and innovative. Ideas come easily to us. Our exchanges with others become powerful. We are able to listen to others, to truly value and utilize the talents and contributions of others. We act in concert with others rather than competing. We remain calm and act with consistency during trying times.

Our minds are clear. We are able to think outside of the box and develop creative solutions. We easily trust intuition and know the best next step to take. We make good decisions and act on them easily and effortlessly. We care. We truly listen and communicate well. We have fun, laugh easily at ourselves, and have a sense of joy and peace, even in difficult circumstances.

We are kind, compassionate, forgiving, and loving to others and to ourselves. We are healthy and vibrant. We sleep well. We make love well. We eat and process our food well. We are filled with energy. We feel free to change without anxiety. We feel free to empower ourselves, raise the bar, and move forward without fear of failure. We are free to encourage the truth, to not make assumptions, to not take things personally, and to have a powerful attitude. We accept good graciously in our lives, and all our needs are met abundantly. We are thankful for all that we are, all that we have, and all of our blessings.

We are free to be our same authentic selves everywhere we go. We are free to use the strengths we have at work in our personal lives and free to use the strengths we have in our personal lives at work.

We fulfill our roles as leaders, followers, team members, partners, managers, employees, spouses, parents, children, siblings, teachers, students, and human beings—professionally and personally.

We make a difference.

We are inspired.

It is always your next move.

—Napoleon Hill

MANAGING THOUGHT

My Dear Friends,

I've always remembered Taoist Master Om Ni Hua Ching saying that we read too many books. He teaches that it is far more effective to read one good book again and again. As we put into practice what we learn, we rise to a new level of consciousness. We gain a deeper understanding as we reread the book from a new perspective at each new level of consciousness.

It is my hope that you choose to reread *Managing Thought* for years to come and use it as a trusted guide, mentor, and mirror. Because each day of living brings new and different experiences, each time you read this book, a new discovery emerges as you sculpt the work of art in progress that is you.

If you would like to learn more about *Managing Thought* or share your discoveries, your challenges, and your triumphs, please visit www.managingthought.com.

Each of us owns the power of thought.
Each of us chooses how to live our lives.
How do your thoughts rule your world?

Enjoy your journey. Enjoy your life well lived.

Mary

*Never doubt
that a small group of
thoughtful, committed citizens
can change the world.
Indeed, it is the only thing
that ever has.*

—Margaret Mead

ACKNOWLEDGMENTS

As I sat down to write the acknowledgments, I reflected on the path of *Managing Thought*, from its inception to the release of the book. I am amazed to see how many people contributed to this one project. The following list does not include all the people who have inspired me or influenced me—whose lessons are also reflected in this book—teachers, advisors, friends, relatives, co-workers, colleagues, children, people I have met on airplanes or while standing in a line, people who have written books I have read, and those who inspired and influenced them. It is endless. It is easy to see how everything we do continues the work of all human ancestors, how connected we are, and how everything we think, say, and do makes a difference.

My heartfelt thanks to:

Ed and Marge Lore, my parents, for bringing me into this world. My mother, for teaching me that practice makes permanent and that you can do anything if you put your mind to it. My father, for teaching me that by admitting we don't know something, and by laughing at ourselves, we open the door to infinite learning.

Gregg Simmons, my departed husband, for his deep love and fine example of a life well lived; for the proof that by being in the moment in each of our moments, we experience infinity; for seeing the love and light in me, holding up the mirror so I could see it too, and encouraging me to share this light with others. Thank you for the honor and joy of being your best friend, lover, confidante, teacher, student, and fellow adventurer. Thank you for your friends, who have become my friends.

Daniel Simmons, my stepson, for your love, your smile, your energy and enthusiasm, your faith and confidence in me, and for the joy and honor of being in your life.

The men and women of TEC and Vistage, for welcoming me to your groups and to your companies, for opening your minds and hearts, and for making self-awareness fun. Thank you for sharing with me your questions, criticisms, challenges, and triumphs. I have learned so much from each of you and I am still learning.

Peggy Beadle, Michael Balloch, and Bob Carrothers for inviting me to your groups, asking the group members to give me feedback, and introducing me to the community as a resource speaker.

Richard Czarnecki, my accounting professor at the University of Michigan-Dearborn, for showing me that one who is true to himself is inspired and inspires many; that significant results are achieved through education, not persuasion; that most of the income earned from doing great service is tax free; and that the whole world doesn't have to be in balance!

Frank Moran, founder of Plante and Moran, for inspiring me to pursue the study of philosophy in addition to finance and accounting, for demonstrating that the culture of a company is what drives results—that when employees are happy and healthy, they perform great service, which helps the customer, who in turn values and rewards the organization, which in turn helps the individual, who performs great service.

To Om Ni Hua Ching, who taught me to value the awakening that is offered by shocks and difficulties; that calmness is significant in dealing with shock and confusion, and necessary in fulfilling great responsibility; that when I am centered, I act appropriately, regardless of what confronts me; and that the power of awe inspires me to cultivate myself and help others.

Bob Nourse, who through the awakening offered by the shock and difficulty of the loss of his own business, received and acted upon the idea to found TEC, also known as Vistage, and through a simple, timeless process, is helping thousands of CEOs and key executives to cultivate themselves and their organizations. I thank Bob for the opportunity and privilege to participate in and continue his dream as a member, chair, coach, mentor, and resource speaker to TEC and Vistage groups around the world.

The University of Michigan-Dearborn, my alma mater, for inviting me to address fellow alumni and speak about what made me successful, and who unknowingly helped me to coin the term *Managing Thought.*

Debbie Oestreich, for encouraging me to share my life and learnings with others, and for helping me to found Managing Thought.

Fellow TEC and Vistage chairs and members: Mary Allan, Peggy Beadle, Laddie and Judy Blaskowski, David Boyette, Steve Brody, Bob Carrothers, Larry Cassidy, Don Clayton, Bob Dabic, Harry Dennis, Lisa Dugan, Ann Ewen, Suzanne Frindt, William Hall Jr., Pat Hyndman, Ozzie Gontang, Arthur Horwitz, Eric Palmaer, Kevin Rafferty, Susan Scott, Jack Sell, Brad Shaffer, Dick Shorten, Diana Sikes, Jaynie Smith, Nick Stavropoulos, Lynn Tanner, Pamela Stambaugh, John Swan, Linda Swindling, Ted Verdery, John Wallingford, Bob Waterloo, and John Younker for reaching out and offering advice, encouragement, and sponsorship when I asked for help from the tribe.

Lisa Cassidy Gautz, for designing my life logo and the artwork for the interior of the book and for her hard work, sacrifice, loyalty, and friendship working with me for all these years.

Michael Balloch, LaTanya Batie, Peggy Beadle, Bill Brunhofer, Tom Buck, Amanda Carrothers, Bob Carrothers, Julia Dingle,

Susan Dockery, Mike Girolami, Jesse Lopez, Janet Macunovich, Karen Malley, Neil Malley, Eric Palmaer, Andrea Rakowicz, Brenda Schulmeister, Larry Short, Gregg Simmons, Debbie Simmons, Barbara Stanbridge, Nick Stavropolous, Joanne Steinwachs, David Ternes, and Peter Wilde, for your time in reading the book and answering thirty-two questions in great detail, and for your thoughtful comments and encouragement.

Fellow Vistage and TEC chairs and members: David Boyette, Larry Cassidy, Bob and Mary Carrothers, Don Clayton, Harry Dennis, Lisa Dugan, Suzanne Frindt, Ozzie Gontang, Pat Hyndman, Louise Levy, Eric Palmeer, Kevin Rafferty, Jack Sell, Dick Shorten, Linda Swindling, John Swan, Ted Verdery, and John Younker for support and encouragement when I asked for help from the tribe.

Chuck Lowery, Kevin McCarthy, David Groppel, Norm Pappas, Michael Balloch, Kim Jugowicz, Eric Palmaer, Joyce Saranathan, Jim Simpson, and Susan Tukel for investing in me.

My editors, Paul Hall, Christine Kane, Jan Jones, Kris Yankee, and John Aherne, my publishers, Ferne Press and McGraw-Hill, and my literary agent, Janet Goldstein, for thoughtful input and for making the process enjoyable. The team at Staples Store #371 in West Bloomfield, Michigan for unbelievably terrific service.

And thank you to those of you who have given me the honor and pleasure of being of service to you.

Mary J. Lore is the founder and CEO of Managing Thought, LLC, which helps individuals and organizations develop self-awareness and change the way they think to attain long-lasting success. She is an internationally recognized leader, executive mentor, and award-winning author.

Mary has devoted thirty years to serving as a CPA, senior executive, turnaround expert, entrepreneur, and mentor to corporate leaders. She has successfully assisted others in North America and Europe through her corporate and public workshops and thousands of hours working with CEOs, managers, employees, teachers, parents, and teens. Since 2002, Mary serves as a chair and expert resource for Vistage International, also known as TEC, the world's preeminent membership organization for the personal and professional development of CEOs.

Managing Thought sprouted from an *aha!* moment when Mary—feeling drained, unhealthy and completely out of balance—realized that she could take responsibility for her reality. She decided to apply the system of thinking and being that made her successful at work to change her entire life.

Mary earned a BBA in finance, with a minor in philosophy, and graduated valedictorian from the University of Michigan-Dearborn. In 1997, she was named Distinguished Alumnus of the Year by the Alumni Society and was the chapter honoree for Beta Gamma Sigma in 2002. She has served on the University of Michigan-Dearborn's College of Business Advisory Board since its inception in 1993. She was named one of Michigan's Top 25 Women Business Owners of Distinction, and her company was named one of metro-Detroit's future 50 companies for three consecutive years.

Mary is certified in Gardening Fine Arts, as well as the practice of Dao-In, an ancient Chinese yoga practice. Mary enjoys camping, hiking, cooking, singing, traveling, and enjoying the company of family and friends. She currently resides in Michigan.

ABOUT MANAGING THOUGHT

*M*anaging Thought helps individuals, families, organizations, and businesses develop self-awareness and change the way they think to achieve long-lasting success.

We provide a step-by-step process to help you become aware of your thoughts, discover what you truly want at work and in life, change your thoughts, and turn what is significant to you into reality.

We believe that practicing *Managing Thought* is the best gift we can give to ourselves, our families, our organizations, our communities, and the world. It is our honor and pleasure to help you manage your thoughts, practice self-awareness, be on purpose be inspired, and change your world.

Copies of the PrioriTree exercises that appear in this book may be downloaded for free at www.managingthought.com.

If you want to learn more about *Managing Thought*, the "How Do Your Thoughts Rule Your World?" self-assessment, and other tools and services we offer, please visit www.managingthought .com.

For inquiries about keynote talks, workshops, consulting, and coaching, visit us at www.managingthought.com.

Mary welcomes your comments, and questions. Her e-mail address is mary@managingthought.com.

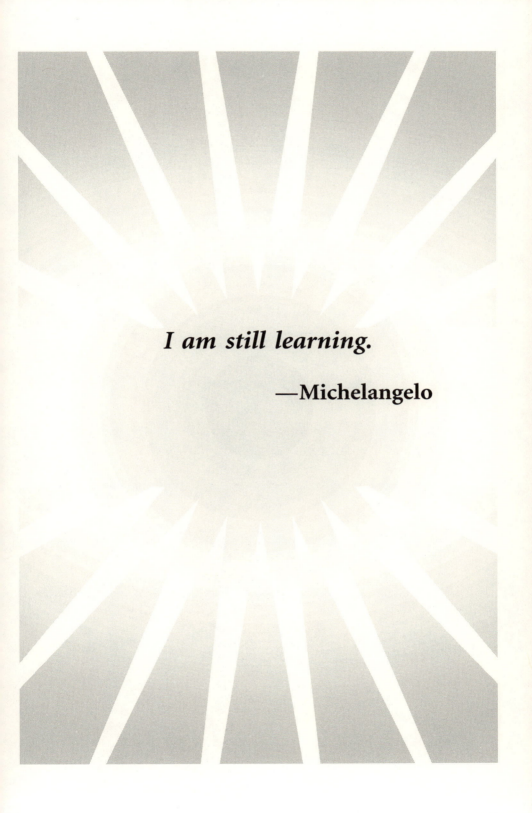

I am still learning.

—Michelangelo